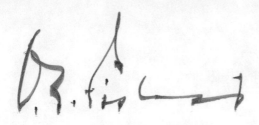

from

N. K. (Doc) & Patty Farmer
F5 Ranch, HC 87, Box 74
Junction, Texas 76849-9705

to

The Institute of Texan Cultures

8/5/89

Western Frontier Library
(Complete list on pages 155–57)

KING FISHER
His Life and Times

KING
FISHER

His Life
and Times

By O. C. Fisher
with J. C. Dykes

UNIVERSITY OF OKLAHOMA PRESS
NORMAN

BY O. C. FISHER

It Occurred in Kimble (Houston, 1937)

Great Western Indian Fights (with others) (Garden City, 1960)

Texas Heritage of the Fishers and the Clarks (Salado, Texas, 1964)

King Fisher: His Life and Times (with J. C. Dykes) (Norman, 1966)

LIBRARY OF CONGRESS CATALOG CARD NUMBER: 66–22719

Copyright 1966 by the University of Oklahoma Press, Publishing Division of the University. Composed and printed at Norman, Oklahoma, U.S.A., by the University of Oklahoma Press. First edition, September, 1966; second printing, March, 1967.

To the memory of Grey (Doc) White, who never claimed a calf that was not following a White brand; a stalwart frontiersman and homesteader who established the first permanent settlement on the Pendencia in Dimmit County.

FOREWORD

WHAT I KNOW ABOUT KING FISHER I learned from my late father, a first cousin of the legendary King, and from talking with people who were contemporaries of the border leader and knew him personally. In addition, I have drawn upon the many reports of his activities written by eyewitnesses and others who either knew him or had other sources of information. Using this material, I have attempted to reconcile the many existing conflicts and record a fair and accurate account of his life and times.

The center of Fisher's operations was his ranch on the Pendencia Creek in Dimmit County, not far from the Río Grande. From that headquarters he carved out an empire during a turbulent period of border history.

"This is King Fisher's road—take the other one." This warning, scribbled on a hewn board, nailed to a tree, appeared in 1876, near King's Pendencia ranch where two crooked wagon trails forked and one angled toward the border leader's headquarters only a few miles away.

The warning was not to be taken lightly. This was King Fisher's Territory, as it had come to be known, and the King was not given to idle boasting or trivial horseplay. The stranger who ignored the veiled warning did not necessarily risk his life, but he was well advised to proceed with caution with no strings attached to his mission. King Fisher did not stand for any foolishness in this part of the country.

But, by strange circumstance, the biggest name on the Mexican border at that time was himself measuring his life and future in terms of which route *he* would take—which road he would follow. Years later he spoke of how that decision haunted him.

The King Fisher story encompasses a decade of Texas border history—a decade which has been called the terrible seventies. Between San Felipe and Brownsville, a distance of seven hundred miles, little evidence of law and order could be detected. On both sides of the Río Grande conditions were intolerable. Cattle thieves, cutthroats, and other outlaws and gamblers and homesteaders wormed their way through the chaparral, all vying for supremacy and survival.

King Fisher, youthful, colorful, and resourceful, moved in to become the dominant figure. With a fast draw, steel courage, irrepressible ambition, and a truly magnetic personality and capacity for leadership, he carved out the empire that made of him a legend.

"The people simply will not let King Fisher die. Eighty years since he was killed he is still a lively topic of conversation when border lore and gunslingers are discussed," according to H. Bailey Carroll, director, Texas State Historical Association.

Despite the hundreds of magazine stories that have been written about Fisher, an air of mystery still surrounds him. Conflicting accounts have been recorded of his career on the border. Some portrayals of his early life have been false and unfounded. For example, the circumstances of his death have been both distorted and ignored. Fisher was not born in Kentucky, contrary to many written accounts; he was born in Texas. It is likely that he never saw the Blue Grass

State. Among other fallacies, historians have said that King's father was killed in a battle with federal troops near Fort Worth, and the father has been pictured as a trouble maker. Actually King's father never fought federal troops except during the Civil War. The elder Fisher was a law-abiding citizen who tried desperately to prevent his oldest son from associating with the Brutons at Goliad—before many of that family migrated to Dimmit County and the border—because he considered the Brutons undesirable and feared they would be a bad influence upon King.

Another inaccurate story, repeated many times, has it that King at the age of sixteen "killed his first man" at Goliad in 1870. Records do not indicate that he was ever accused of killing anyone in Goliad County. Biographers of gunmen evidently feel that killings by their heroes while very young add greatly to their reputations. Legend has it that Billy the Kid killed his first man at the age of twelve.

These are but a few of the misconceptions bandied about concerning this noted border character. One of the nation's top gunslingers, Fisher completely dominated an area of more than five thousand square miles along the Mexican border for several years during the turbulent 1870's. His unique qualities brought him to a position of dominance during an unsettled era along the Río Grande when men made and enforced their own law.

King Fisher was the product of the post-Civil War period which spawned scores of gunfighters who left an imprint upon the history of the times. That era covered about four decades—from the 1860's to the turn of the century. These forty years were a period of transition, including Recon-struction, when America was grudgingly turning from old ways to new. New frontier settlements were being made, and social restrictions were beginning to take form.

If Thomas Carlyle is right, and history is to a large extent biography, then a study of gunmen of this era is revealing. Such men were known on the cattle trails and in the mining camps. They were often seen at Dodge, Abilene, Cheyenne, Caldwell, and at Hays City.

It has been said that the story of the gunman is the story of the frontier. Not all of it, but when we add the record of the men with whom the gunman dealt, the environment he made or influenced, and his female companions and those of his associates, the story of the gunman is very much the story of the West as it unfolded during that epochal period.

When the gunfighter era began, the Civil War was raging. At the close of that conflict, with the agonizing readjustments which followed, there were scores of young men, restless and bold, armed and eager to show their mettle. Only in the frontier settlements on the prairies of Canada, where mounted police were already stationed, was there any semblance of law and order for early arrivals.

It was under these circumstances and in that environment that gunfighters made the most of the freedom that was theirs. Among their number were robbers, thieves, gamblers, killers, and other dangerous characters. And from among them also emerged top law-enforcement officers, such as Wild Bill Hickok, Bat Masterson, and others—including King Fisher.

While some lawmen left their profession to engage in illegal activities, the reverse was true of the King. He stands out as an example of one who engaged in lawlessness in a wild, lawless border country, then reformed and established an enviable record as a top law enforcer at a time when the duties of peace officers were dangerous and demanding.

The more noted the gunman, the more cunning he had

to be. Once the slinger acquired a reputation, he was a shining target, and he knew it. As an example, Wild Bill Hickok, when he relaxed his vigilance sitting at a gambling table in Deadwood, was murdered by a sneaking and rank amateur, Jack McCall, in 1876.

A study of the lives of famous gunmen reveals their adherence to a code of ethics when it came to killing. While there were cowardly gunslingers, who "never gave a sucker a chance," the most prominent of them were not inclined to take unfair advantage. When they killed they wanted to face their adversary, and they wanted him armed. The more respected gunman, when he intended to kill another man, was never disposed to shoot an unarmed opponent or fire from ambush. He was at his best face to face with an adversary with lightning speed when split seconds, a dead aim, and cool nerve meant the difference between life and death.

It is estimated there were as many as 250 "bad men" of the West, of different shades, during the gunslinger era— including both peace officers and outlaws. In the struggle to stay alive none of them were good insurance risks. Rarely did one of them live beyond forty; Ben Thompson reached forty-one, but Billy the Kid died at twenty-one, and the average was on the order of thirty years.

Jack Thorp expressed it this way:

> *These were frontier towns, ol' pardner;*
> *Twas a game o' take an' give*
> *An' the one who could draw the fastest*
> *Was the only one who'd live!*

King Fisher was a product of that period. In his own area his influence was awesome, his personality dominant. He has become a legendary character. It is not easy to confirm many of the stories that have been told about him, and undoubtedly there are many exaggerations. Interwoven as the story of his life is with that of the Nueces Strip—along the border—during the wildest era ever experienced on the Río Grande, where records are faulty and often obscure, one can only piece the fragments of history together in an effort to reconstruct his behavior and do justice to his conduct.

O. C. FISHER

Washington, D.C.
June 28, 1966

xiv

ACKNOWLEDGMENTS

I AM INDEBTED to many people for assistance in the preparation of this volume. Mrs. Verna Linburg, former superintendent of schools of Goliad County, was particularly helpful in research concerning early-day events there. Lizzie and Carrie Taylor, also of Goliad, part-owners and present occupants along with their brother of The Old Rock House, built by Lloyd Vivian 120 years ago, shared with me their storehouse of knowledge concerning Goliad pioneers. In 1935 King Fisher's widow and her sister, along with Judge Terrell Kellogg, a grandson of King Fisher, visited the old place, and these sisters recalled for me the widow's nostalgic recollections of her childhood in the Vivian house.

Jeff C. Dykes, himself an eminent historian, helped me collect source material and plan the manuscript.

Kellogg's sister, Mrs. Maurine Gardner, of Carrizo Springs, Texas, was very helpful in supplying data relating to her grandfather and the family. Her son, the Honorable Pat Gardner, of San Antonio, added to this information.

Others who provided information or otherwise assisted include: Mrs. Florence Finley, of Uvalde, Texas; Warren Pulliam, of Crystal City, Texas; Judge Paul Kilday, of Washington, D.C.; the Honorable Herbert Petry, Jr., of Carrizo Springs; J. H. Newcomer, of Uvalde; Ben E. Pingenot, of Eagle Pass; Paul Adams, historian and authority on King Fisher, of San Antonio; the Honorable David Hume, E. H. Schmidt, and Mr. and Mrs. Ben White, all of Carrizo Springs; George W. Baylor, of Tucson, Arizona; H. Bailey Carroll, director, Texas State Historical Association; the late Honorable Robert T. Neill, of San Angelo; the Honorable Charles T. Halton, of San Antonio; Dorman H. Winfrey, state librarian, and James E. Day, state archivist, and the following district clerks: A. Rene Barrientos, of Eagle Pass, Paul S. Cluck, of Laredo, and Mrs. Beulah Barber, of Uvalde.

I am particularly indebted to my late father, Jobe Fisher, who was an acquaintance and first cousin of King Fisher. Thirty years ago my father dictated to me many details about the family and King's early life.

O. C. FISHER

CONTENTS

KING FISHER
His Life and Times

I

King Fisher's Early Life

WHO WAS KING FISHER and what was his background? What heredity, environment, and other influences could have helped fashion his remarkable and meteoric career and make him a legendary figure in the annals of the Southwest?

King Fisher was born in 1854, of humble parentage. King's father, Joby Fisher (later known as Jobe), was born in Arkansas, where his father James Fisher, Sr., had stopped over for a few years while en route from Illinois to Texas—then a part of Mexico. The latter crossed into Santa Anna's northernmost province in 1835. In failing health, he traveled only fifty miles into Texas before stopping to build a log house and carve out a homestead on Sister Grove Creek in what was then Fannin County, later renamed Collin County.

The senior Fisher had married Anna Ladd, resident of Virginia but a native of Holland. He died in 1837, before he could enjoy the fruits of his exciting venture into a new country.

Following the death of her husband, Anna and the children claimed a league and labor of land from the new Republic of Texas, and it was granted. In two tracts, the 4,605 acres were located on Sister Grove Creek. When the children reached maturity they were given proportionate shares of the acreage. The oldest child, Jobe, was the widowed mother's favorite, and she deeded him additional land from her one-half interest in the grants. He later purchased more of her share.

Jobe married Lucinda Warren, a native of Kentucky and daughter of Hiram Warren, member of a family prominent in Collin County at the time. Lucinda's brother, Cam, one of her five brothers and sisters, later became a storekeeper at McKinney, Texas.

Two children were born to Jobe and Lucinda—John King (subject of this sketch) and Jasper. The mother died at the birth of the second child, and following the custom of the times, Jobe soon remarried. Cam Warren, displeased with Jobe's second wife, requested Jobe to let him rear and educate John King and Jasper. Fisher bluntly rejected the offer, however, insisting that he was quite capable of rearing his own family.

Just before the Civil War, Jobe moved his family to Florence in Williamson County. In October of 1861, he enlisted in the military and was attached to Captain J. L. Whittenberg's infantry company from Williamson County, Twenty-seventh Brigade, commanded by General E. S. C. Robertson.

Military records reveal that on April 2, 1863, Jobe was attached to a mounted company of the Minute Men, Twenty-first Brigade, under the command of General William Hudson, then in charge of Texas State Troops. Afterwards he was transferred to the Confederate States Army before being mustered out on February 1, 1864.

Returning to Florence at the end of the war, Jobe remained there but a short time. His second wife, Minerva, was in failing health, and soon he took her and the children to Lampasas to make use of the springs there, then considered to have health-restoring qualities.

The Fisher family were primitive or "hard shell" Baptists. They were very religious people, and in the rearing of the children they were strict disciplinarians, as is indicated by an incident that happened while the Jobe Fishers were living at Florence at the end of the war.

The author's father (also named Jobe, and son of James Fisher, Jr.), Jasper, Kelp Queen, and Tom Van Hook went to Joe Whittenberg's to pick wild plums from a grove, taking along gourds for containers. When Mrs. Whittenberg only gave them a few plums to eat, the kids were disappointed because she was not more generous, and on their return trip my father and Jasper slipped into the plum thicket to fill their gourds.

Mrs. Whittenberg, alert and suspicious, had followed the youngsters, and she surprised Jasper in the act—my father had concealed himself inside the thicket. Mounting a surprise attack, she whammed Jasper with an empty bucket; then she sternly ordered him off the premises. Upon their return home the boys reported what had happened, thinking the incident was very funny.

"To my surprise," my father told me, "my Uncle Jobe did not see the funny side of it at all and lectured Jasper on the gravity of the offense of taking other people's property, and proceeded to give him a good thrashing."

In 1865 King's father owned several hundred head of cattle. These were moved to Lampasas, where good cattle range abounded. Aside from the attraction of its springs as a health feature, Lampasas was then a cow village at the edge of the frontier and a trading and outfitting post where ranchers came to get their supplies. Jobe, tempted to settle

5

there, probably would have but for the state of his wife's health. A doctor recommended a lower climate for her, preferably in a coastal area.

A few months later the Fishers moved to Goliad, a bustling community in South Texas. There Fisher established a home, and aside from his cattle business he began operating freight wagons from Powder Horn, an old boat landing forty miles below Goliad, up toward central Texas.

About one year later, when King was only thirteen years of age, a Goliad frontiersman named Grey (Doc) White, a friend of the Fisher family, led a wagon train of settlers and their cattle herds west toward the Mexican border country. King wanted to go along but was too young. Instead, his father sent him on another mission.

"It was about 1869," my father recalled, "that Uncle Jobe sent King from Goliad to Florence to live with us and go to school. In the meantime, Jobe's second wife had died. He had two children by her—John and Laura. Jasper was then driving one of the freight wagons with his father, and King, John and their little sister were left to look after their home at Goliad and see about the cattle. Grandma Fisher went down there to help them. I recall that Uncle Jobe sent word that King was being thrown in contact with some very questionable people, named Brutons, and he was quite concerned about their influence over the young man. King rode alone on a sorrel mule from Goliad to our home in Florence, about 150 miles."

My father described King as a handsome young man, with square shoulders and a manly bearing. A good student, he was rather quiet and mild-mannered. He was, however, good at fist fighting and usually got the best end of all the fights he had with youngsters in the neighborhood. Always

6

popular with the girls, King was often seen with them at the frequent camp meetings of that time.

"I remember very well the time King whipped Ed Burns," my father recalled. "Ed and my sister Annie were going together. One night a dance was going on at Sam Queen's."

He then told of how King, "Little King" (a son of Jesse Fisher's and a second cousin of King's), Ed Burns, and John Stevenson all came to the dance together. Burns was bruised about the face and had got the injuries, according to the boys, from his horse's running under a limb with him. But at her insistence "Little King" told Annie what had actually happened. He confided to her that as they were coming out of town that afternoon a horse race was matched, the aftermath of which was a fist fight between King and Ed. There had been a little wager on the race.

King, though then only fifteen years of age, was an unusually good rider. He bought and swapped horses in the neighborhood and made it a practice to trade for the wildest animals in the community, then ride and break them. He was considered one of the top bronc riders around Florence at the time.

A few months later King had his first scrape with the law. He had been up for two or three nights and while riding along one afternoon became sleepy. He unsaddled and was taking a nap under a shade when his horse pulled away and left.

When King found the horse missing, he put his bridle on a stallion belonging to a Mr. Turnbow so that he could chase his pony. He didn't take time to ask permission, since he was in a hurry and he was friendly with the Turnbows, including the two sons—Hugh and Bill. He captured his horse, then turned the stallion loose where he had found him without reporting to Turnbow what he had done.

Turnbow found out what had happened. Several people in the community had seen King riding the stallion. The owner, quite proud of his horse, proceeded to file a complaint against King for using the steed without the owner's consent. When the young man heard that he was "wanted" by the constable he made up his mind to avoid arrest. A number of men were obtained to search for him, one of them being Arch Ratliff, a relative of King's.

"I recall," continued my father, "that a day or two later King rode up to our house and said, 'Aunt Nancy, fix me up some food; I'm going to leave the country.' Us children led the horse around the house and were feeding him. King said he was figuring on going back to Goliad soon anyhow, that school was out, and he might as well go ahead. As he ate, my mother fixed him some food to take along.

"My mother was fond of King and was sympathetic toward him. I have heard her tell about King's step-mother hanging King up by the suspenders to the top of a doorway when he was a little child, there to kick and struggle while she did the household chores."

As King was eating, a number of horsemen were observed coming in the distance. The young man mounted his pony and made his getaway. That was his last appearance at my grandfather's home.

He was captured the next morning, some seven or eight miles away, as he slept in the woods, his horse staked nearby. The prisoner was taken before the justice of the peace, and Constable Ike Barber, King, and Turnbow were sent by horseback to Georgetown, the county seat, some fifteen miles away.

In the meantime Turnbow had regretted his hasty action but, having gone this far with it and having created such a disturbance in the community, he would not drop the charge. King's horse was being led by the constable. While riding alongside King, Turnbow slipped a pocketknife to him. Fisher then cut the lead rope as Barber, astride his horse, drank water from a pail which had just been handed up to him by a woman whose house they were passing. The escaped prisoner made his way back to Goliad and never returned to Florence.

II

Goliad

GOLIAD, a historic site in Texas, was a crossroads community at the end of the Civil War. Rich in Texas history, Goliad was first settled in 1749 after the presidio La Bahía was constructed on the banks of the San Antonio River. La Bahía, which grew into one of the most important forts on the Spanish frontier, served as a landmark and a rallying point for the Anglo-Americans while they built up resistance to the Spanish regime and, later, to the self-styled Napoleon of the West—Santa Anna.

The Goliad Declaration of Independence was contrived at La Bahía early in 1836, and, of course, the infamous Goliad Massacre took place nearby on March 27 of that year.

During the decade following the Civil War, Goliad became the business and commercial hub of a wide area. Many new settlers arrived, travelers stopped over, and the criminal element flocked in to set the stage for a violent struggle with law and order. Cattle raising thrived as herds were made up for movements on the trail. Rustlers were active, and violence erupted almost daily as the inevitable clashes occurred.

The town was on a boom. To meet the demands, several small hotels, livery stables, wagon yards, and mercantile establishments were opened. During the seventies Taylor's Hotel offered upper and lower Sample Rooms for commercial salesmen. The Case Hotel competed by including a stable with fodder and hay to attract patrons. Neyland and Sanderfur specialized in carriages, wagons, and wagon equipment. C. O. Carstens advertised his services as a coffin and cistern maker. L. A. Maetze and Brothers sold staples and fancy groceries, dry goods, and hardware, and H. V. Wideman erected a broom factory. Along with this there were the doctors, lawyers, and the inevitable saloons and gambling houses.

It was into this environment that Jobe Fisher moved his family and his herd about 1866, the year before Doc White organized a wagon train for a move to Dimmit County. Being energetic and ingenious, Fisher saw a need for freighting facilities to supply the Goliad merchants, as well as other frontier trading posts. He acquired two freight wagons and developed a rather lucrative business between the coast and the ready customers in the interior.

Jobe Fisher was right—it was not a very desirable place to rear a family, particularly since the father had to be away from home a good part of the time. After the death of his second wife, his mother—Anna—came down to keep house for him. King was a restless, eager youngster, and even during his early years he associated with some of the rougher element in the community. The father, deeply concerned about this, was prompted to send King to Florence to attend school, hoping to separate him from the bad influence of his companions.

Among the undesirables were members of the Bruton families. Their names appear frequently on the criminal records at Goliad, and before the seventies came along some of them had sought greener and more secluded fields in Maverick and Dimmit counties.

One of the leading and more respected citizens living

11

in Goliad when Jobe Fisher moved there was Caroline, the widow of Lloyd Vivian. She and her husband had moved there in 1839, fresh from the remains of Jean Laffite's colony at Galveston.

Vivian first built a log house atop a grass-covered hill. The next year he began work on a rock structure, using slave labor from the cart trail, working part time between trips. Limestone was quarried from the hill, and mortar was made by burning limestone dust in a kiln. Cypress for windows and floors was shipped up the cart trail from Indianola. It took several years to complete the new house, a big handsome four-room structure with a fireplace in each room. The log cabin in the back was converted into a kitchen, and other cabins down the hill were outfitted for slaves.

Vivian omitted windows from the west side of the house and left a blank wall, probably for two reasons. In the first place, the storms sweeping across the prairie from the Gulf would have banged the wooden window shutters, and secondly, it meant one less side to guard against marauding Indians.

The Old Rock House, as it was called, that Lloyd Vivian built has attracted the attention of passers-by almost as much as the ancient missions and battlefields of the historic old town, and it stands as a landmark today, a silent monument to the sturdy workmanship and vision and pride of the builder, Lloyd Vivian [*Houston Chronicle*, Nov. 7, 1958].

The widow sold the old house and the one-thousand-acre tract upon which it stood to Shadwick White. White sold the house to D. R. Fant, a wealthy cattleman, who in 1882 sold it to Joseph Taylor, a relative of General Zachary Taylor, of Mexican War fame and President of the United

States. Still owned by Taylor descendants, the house is now occupied by Sheaper, Lizzie, and Carrie Taylor.

John, one of Lloyd's sons, married Jane O'Neal. Their daughter Sarah, born in 1847, later became the wife of King Fisher. Sarah was born in an old log house, on the premises where the Lloyd Vivian house was located. She and King began their childhood wooing in the Old Rock House, then the central point for the social activities of the Vivians and their friends.

Years later, in 1935, two of Jane's daughters, Mrs. Maggie Ware and Mrs. King Fisher, accompanied by the latter's grandson, Terrell Kellogg, went back to Goliad to visit the Old Rock House. John Vivian, father of these two, died in 1895 in a mishap with a horse. His widow lived to celebrate her one hundredth birthday before she passed away. In her later life she made her home with her daughter, Mrs. King Fisher, in Carrizo Springs.

Amid brush and cactus enclosed by a cast-iron fence on the old homestead, are the graves of Lloyd and Caroline Vivian. Between the two lies Frank, born August 24, 1841, died October 8, 1866. Caroline was born December 28, 1817, and died March 17, 1902, her body having been brought back to the old home place for interrment beside that of her husband. Lloyd's birth date is shown as January 12, 1819, and he expired March 17, 1863.

When King Fisher returned to Goliad, following a few months spent at Florence, he soon resumed his old associations. King's father and Jasper were away most of the time, and there was not much for King to do in a town crowded with strangers, including an assortment of gamblers and outlaws. His unhappy experiences of escaping from the posse at Florence and slipping away from the constable who had him under arrest helped to encourage a childhood resistance to law and order.

It was not long before King was hauled into court at Goliad, charged, along with an older man—Willis Fulcord—with housebreaking. On October 5, 1870, indictments were returned against the two—a part of a massive indignation drive then taking place to rid Goliad of its criminal element. In fact, at the same term of court when these two indictments were returned there were a total of seventy-six indictments filed. Feeling was running high against every suspect, and sixteen-year-old King was caught in the determined drive.

Two days after King was indicted he made $500 bond, with Richard Vivian and Charles Bruton serving as sureties. Fisher's case was called for trial on the same day, and a search of court records discloses neither an application for continuance nor a request for a suspended sentence. He pleaded "not guilty," but a jury gave him two years in the penitentiary. Fulcord got five years.

Four days later young Fisher's motion for a new trial was overruled, he accepted sentence, and it was "ordered by the court that the sheriff be allowed three persons, to-wit, W. C. Cartwright, George Simmons, and C. Q.Ragland, to go as a guard in conveying the prisoners Willis Fulcord and King Fisher to the penitentiary at Huntsville."

Both prisoners were received at Huntsville, on October 30. Prison records contain this description of the youngest of the arrivals. Age 16; height, 5-9; weight, 135; complexion, fair; hair, brown; education, not given; occupation, laborer.

While it must be assumed that King was guilty of the crime with which he was charged, he having been duly indicted and convicted, there were obviously extenuating

14

circumstances which apparently were not advanced during the trial or were ignored by the jury.

In any event, after less than four months in prison, the young man was given a full pardon by the governor, reportedly because of his youth. Fulcord died in prison November 14, 1874.

Back in Goliad, hardened by prison life, alert, ambitious, and determined, King could see no future in what he considered an unfriendly community. He missed his friends who had gone to the Pendencia in Dimmit County. He learned that Charles Bruton, who had helped make his bond, had already departed for the border—just ahead of the sheriff who had warrants for his arrest. In fact, on June 9, 1871, when the next grand jury met, Bruton was indicted at Goliad for using an unrecorded brand, for violating the estray law, and also for seduction and rape. Warrants for his arrest were sent to Maverick, Uvalde, and Medina counties but apparently they were never served.

By this time King had heard from Doc White, and in company with Bud Thompson the seventeen-year-old cowboy saddled his pony, bade his father adieu, and headed for the Pendencia. King left behind his father and two brothers. His sister Laura apparently had passed away, since there is no mention of her in the 1870 census report. His father is presumed to have died shortly thereafter.

The last evidence of Jobe's presence at Goliad, or elsewhere, is found in the record there of a bill of sale which he executed on December 5, 1870, when in consideration of $190 he sold, range delivery, thirty-seven head of stock cattle to W. W. Bruton.

It had been three years since Doc White left Goliad. King's memory went back to that occasion. He recalled that as a thirteen-year-old boy he had ridden out to the White camp the first night after their departure from the town, persisting in his desire to join the westward move.

"That's a man's country," Doc White had ruled. "We'll have enough to do without taking care of another kid."

III

From Goliad to the Pendencia

GREY (DOC) WHITE had been the leader of that group of migrants pushing westward seeking homesites in new country. He had moved to Goliad at the end of the Civil War. A native of Jackson County, Texas, he had been attracted to the West, and Goliad, then a thriving frontier trading post, had been his first stop. At Goliad he met Louisa Jane Osgood, an attractive young widow with two children— James and Albert, the latter an infant at the time. A brief courtship ensued, and they were married in 1866.

White, called "Doc" because he was an amateur veterinarian, soon heard about the attractions afforded by the unsettled Pendencia Creek area in Dimmit County, not far from the Mexican border. Confederate troops had patrolled the lush prairies of that area during the war. Among them were Captain Levi English, John Burleson, and Charles and Blue Vivian, all Goliad residents. At the conclusion of hostilities these scouts returned to their old home to tell of the tall grass, running brooks, and scenic grandeur of the Pendencia country. It did not take much selling to convince Doc White that Pendencia was the place for him.

White then proceeded to organize a wagon train of Goliad residents, most prominent of whom were members of the Vivian family. Lloyd Vivian's widow, Caroline, headed that family group, which included James, Bill, La-

17

Fayette, Dick and Wesley Vivian, and the Vivians' Negro servant, Simon Love. LaFayette had married Ordania, a sister of Doc White's. Others who joined the caravan included French Struther and John Gibson.

On the first night out, when King had joined them briefly, the families gathered around the campfire, talking of the past and the future. Suspense and anxiety flashed on every face as Indian raids and clashes with border ruffians were anticipated. Their thoughts were of new adventure, a new life in a new world, of what lay over the horizon, two hundred miles to the west. Winter had set in, and the campfire was comforting as Doc White warned them ominously of what to expect.

"I want to get away from driving oxen and raising cotton," Doc allowed, adding a note of plausibility to his reasons for courting trouble as a price for a new home in a new country. There was a ripple of approval among the women and children who huddled around the smoking embers.

The herd of cattle bawled restlessly as the men took their turns during the night to keep them from drifting. A lot of cattle stealing was going on in Goliad County, and the owners were taking no chances. They were determined to move the herd slowly and arrive at their destination with a minimum of losses.

Doc's surviving son, Ben, who now ranches near Carrizo Springs, recalls hearing his father tell about the move and the first night on the trail.

"There were tears in little King's eyes the next morning when the wagon train broke camp and headed west," Doc recalled years later.

"If you run into anything over there you can't handle," bragged King, "just send for me."

18

A youthful courtship that had developed between young King and Sarah, an attractive daughter of John Vivian's, made the parting more difficult for King and added a romantic touch to the parting. They had romped and played together as they met at the palatial Lloyd Vivian home where Lloyd's widow, Caroline, lived near Goliad. Sarah was Caroline's granddaughter. King's childhood interest in Sarah was one reason for his determination to join the settlers at the first opportunity.

The new settlers arrived on the Pendencia (called Pendench) on Christmas Day, 1867. Houses, or *jacales* (called "harkells") were built, with thatched roofs, later replaced with some rock structures to better protect them against the hazard of fire and the Indian depredators who made frequent nocturnal forays during full moons. The Pendencia, then a running stream, was a ready source of water for the families.

Copied from huts of the Mexican pastores, the *jacales* had walls made of straight posts or pickets of mesquite or of elm which grew along the creek banks. These were set in the ground and lashed together with rawhide or Spanish dagger thongs. Split pickets or smaller branches were wedged between the posts. Caliche mixed with sand was used for plastering the walls inside. The roofs were made of *sacahuisto* (salt grass), a water-repellent grass that grew in abundance along the creeks. Deerskins or cowhides were hung over the doors and windows. The floors were hard, of caliche or earth.

This was Doc White's new home, and he had made up his mind to stay. One of the most honored and respected men who ever moved to that area, White was scrupulously honest. He was one of the few who refused to brand a range calf unless it was following a cow bearing the proper brand.

19

On the Pendencia he was a busy, energetic citizen, leading, comforting, and inspiring the neighbors to dig in and make a go of their new location.

"I have more respect for an energetic horse thief than for a lazy honest man," he told them.

White was a community leader all his life. Later he became the first county commissioner from his precinct when Dimmit County was organized in 1880, and he served on the first grand jury empaneled there. He died in Carrizo Springs in 1915.

The new Dimmit settlers were hard pressed to hold on. The county, then unorganized, was attached to Maverick County, of which Eagle Pass was the county seat, for judicial purposes. Organized law enforcement was almost nonexistent.

The frontiersmen thus became their own protectors, enforcing their own laws as best they could. The triple threat menace of Indians, cattle thieves, and Mexican bandits plagued the new settlement, and many of their cattle were stolen.

IV

Dimmit County

DIMMIT COUNTY WAS NAMED for Philip Dimmit, a Pennsylvania adventurer who came to Texas prior to the Texas Revolution. He took part in a number of Texan-Mexican skirmishes in the Goliad area, and he later lived on the Nueces River above Corpus Christi. Captured by Mexicans and taken to Saltillo he is reported [see Webb's, *A Handbook of Texas*] to have committed suicide rather than face torture and death at the hands of his Mexican captors.

The county was carved out of Bexar County by act of the state legislature in 1858.

The White-Vivian settlement, destined to become the future headquarters of King Fisher, was by no means the first settlement in that area. In fact, before Texas gained its independence the Spaniards had made thrusts into the area, and land-grant inducements had been issued, but efforts to settle were sporadic prior to the late fifties and early sixties.

Even before permanent settlements began to dot the prairies following the Civil War, the area was frequented by Indians and visited by Mexican and American mustang hunters [see items by Taylor, Williams, and Wilcox, cited in bibliography].

Traversing the county through the site of Catarina was El Camino Real, which led through Presidio crossing on the river in Maverick County, to San Antonio and the Sabine Pass. Trade moved over this trail, mainly in ox carts, until early in the 1880's. Peloncilla, Spanish blankets, hemp-hair ropes and halters, and other products were brought from Mexico, and corn, rock salt, clothing, and merchandise were taken back.

Those carts, hardy and quaint, bore the brunt of freight traffic for decades on both sides of the Río Grande. Handmade, the two wheels stood originally seven feet in height and seven feet apart. The bed, which was six feet wide and fifteen feet long, was framed out of heavy timbers firmly secured to the pecan or live-oak axle by wooden pins and rawhide thongs. The tongue, which projected twelve feet in front, formed the centerpiece for bed and passed over the axle and both ends of the frame, at which points it was also secured by wooden pins and thongs. Other pieces formed the bed, which was covered by a thatched roof of straw that was supported by heavy standards set in the frame.

Later the crude vehicles were made smaller and improved, drawn by only three yoke of oxen, before the advent of iron tires, which made possible an even smaller wheel. The screeching noise from the wheels' rotating over the axle was described by freighters as "excruciating." A remedy for the noise was prickly pear leaves. Shoved in one at a time, the leaves served as a lubricant when they crushed against the axle [Santleben, *A Texas Pioneer*].

As mule-drawn wagons were developed to gradually replace the carts, bitter competition was engendered which caused serious disturbances, known as the "cart war." The State took a hand in quelling this argument.

Early Dimmit settlers found the country free of brush, except along streams, and the prairies were covered with

22

fine grasses, upon which cattle fattened without extra feeding. Wild game was said to be plentiful, including turkeys, deer, wolves, panthers, *javelin* hogs, and others. In fact, in hard times the settlers hunted *javelinas*, selling the skins for leather and often using the hides as a medium of exchange.

The first attempt at permanent settlement in the county was made shortly before the Civil War by John Townsend, a Negro from Nacogdoches. He and others settled on Pendencia Creek, but in the face of Indian incursions they moved on to the Río Grande above Eagle Pass. Still another settlement was attempted on San Lorenzo Creek by people from Milwaukee. The ruins of their abandoned ranch houses still stand just across the county line in Webb County (Taylor).

The White settlement was preceded by Captain Levi English, who in 1865 brought some four hundred immigrants to Carrizo Springs, only a few of whom stayed. In fact, the census of 1870 showed a population in Dimmit County of only 109 people. That figure did not include many of the drifters who were too elusive for a head count. English, one of the County's leading citizens, later operated a store at Carrizo Springs. Later he bought a section of land, the William Lane Survey, for $220 in silver. It was on this land that Carrizo Springs was laid out by a surveyor named John A. Barnes. Levi deeded land for the public square on which to build a courthouse "and a drinking fountain," and he also gave land to be used for alleys and streets in the new town.

This pioneer's wife, Matilde Burleson English, served as a midwife for the community. Her Negro servant was named Cecilia—given to Matilde as a wedding present in Grimes County in 1838.

23

Another prominent settler and merchant was Samuel Hayes Kellogg. He moved to Carrizo from Pennsylvania and served as postmaster in the new town, sorting the mail for settlers in the post office which was then located in his mercantile store. He married Margaret Rea, a step-daughter of Frank Williams who had brought his family in from Atascosa. Margaret's sister, Sarah, married F. Vandervoort, an attorney and community leader. Years later Kellogg's son, Frank, married Florence Fisher—King Fisher's oldest daughter.

Bud Thompson, who made the trip to Dimmit with King, built a house near the Nueces River and enclosed a pasture between the river and the Espantosa Lake, using skeleton fences and brush. Associated with Thompson was a man named McElroy, who worked with Thompson and used his enclosure to make up herds to take up the trail.

The history of Dimmit is marked by frequent Indian incursions. Lipans, Kiowas, Comanches, and Apaches were the tribes who raided in the Dimmit communities. Later, after most of the tribes were herded into reservations, renegade savages who had escaped into Mexico often raided settlements on the Texas side of the border. In 1878, Lieutenant John Bullis, then in command of the Seminole Scouts and stationed at Fort Clark, told a congressional committee about five bands of Indians who for several years had operated out of sanctuaries in Mexico. These he described as Lipans and Mescalero Apaches.

The Pendencia settlement was subjected to many of these encounters with the redskins. Six months before White's arrival two of Captain English's sons, Ed and Joel, encountered seven Indians while they were out hunting horses. They killed one of the Indians in the ensuing skirmish, and Ed was wounded with a steel-tipped arrow.

In 1870 a band of two hundred Comanches swooped down on the ranch of Charles Vivian, killed a Mexican, and captured a Mexican boy. They also killed Dave Adams, a rancher, and then turned their attention to a cluster of *jacales* at Carrizo Springs.

On another occasion Charles Vivian had one of his leggings pierced by an arrow as he rushed into his ranch home on the Pendencia. A moment later an Indian brave approached the house and was fired upon by Vivian from a window. The bullet penetrated the attacker's leg and killed the horse he was riding. Other Indians ran to the rescue and dragged the wounded comrade away.

Doc White fought Indians repeatedly and was shot through the hand on one occasion.

To better cope with this constant danger, citizens of Carrizo Springs combined with those who lived on the Pendencia, and others, to organize scouting parties. Captain Refugio Benavides, of Laredo, famous on the frontier, aided by State troops, helped.

The settlers were also assisted by the presence of federal troops, under Lieutenant John Bullis, a famous border foe of the Indians, who scouted the area during the seventies and for a time maintained a camp of colored troopers not far from Carrizo Springs.

In his testimony before a congressional committee in 1878, Bullis gave a detailed account of the extent and nature of these depredations. He told of two raids in 1876 and of two more incursions the next year. Twenty-seven men and women had been killed, and cattle, horses, and various plunder had been taken.

Usually afoot and wearing soft moccasins, the depredators, in groups of two up to thirty or forty, left no tracks as they made their way stealthily through cedar breaks and the chaparral, striking by moonlight in the Pendencia area, there stealing and riding horses into Kimble, Kerr, Gillespie, Uvalde, and Maverick counties and surrounding environs.

Yielding to the perils of both Indian marauders and Mexican bandits, many settlements that sprang up in the valleys of the Frio and Sabinal, the Nueces, and other mountain streams, were virtually abandoned [45 Cong., 2 sess., *House Misc. Doc. 64*].

These combined incursions led to an appeal being made to Washington by the Texas Constitutional Convention in 1875 to rush aid to the Río Grande. A commission did go to the border and investigate. A report filed in February, 1876, described conditions along the Río Grande as intolerable. It recommended that the raiders be pursued across the river by U.S. troops, when in "hot pursuit." Another commission had previously looked into the same situation in 1872 and again in 1873.

"The cattle thieves are today," they reported on June 30, 1873, "far more active than last year."

The commission said cattle herds on the Texas side of the border had been decreased by one-fourth their number by Indian and Mexican thieves. Also, 25 per cent of the hides transported northward through the Brownsville customs station bore Texas brands, and another 25 per cent looked like the brands had been altered. The report gave the estimate that cattlemen had suffered losses worth $27,859,-363 and insisted that the Mexican government either shared in the plunder or condoned the thefts [45 Cong., 2 sess., *House Misc. Doc. 64* and other sources cited in bibliography].

According to the report, Mexican local authorities—military and civil—as a rule had been cognizant of these outrages and had protected the offenders, often defeating with technical objections attempts at recovery of the stolen property. They had even assisted in maintaining bands of thieves and directly and openly dealt in the plunder or appropriated it to their personal use.

The United States formally protested to Mexico. The Mexicans sent a commission to the border, and it reported the U.S. claims were exaggerated; that Texans had stolen horses from them; that Indians had been pushed into Mexico by the Americans, and therefore the gringoes caused it; and that the few Mexicans who stole were "trained to this disgraceful practice by Americans."

The Mexican commission then added insult to injury by claiming the American protest was made as an excuse for plans to annex a portion of northern Mexico.

Thus, Indian depredations and cattle stealing combined to make life on the Pendencia uncertain and prosperity impossible. More help was needed if the settlement was to survive. Faced with this dilemma, Doc White thought of King Fisher, who had said, three years before, "If you run into anything over there you can't handle, just send for me."

Word was sent back to Goliad that young King would have a job if he came. The stage was set for the arrival of this rash young man who was destined to play a stellar role in the struggle for survival and to become the most colorful, the most respected, and the most feared man in border history. Indeed he was to become the master of the fates and fortunes of those who chose to reside in the environs of Maverick, Dimmit, Zavalla, and Frio counties, and to wield a powerful influence from Laredo to Eagle Pass, from Oakville to Carrizo Springs. In King Fisher Territory this young man's word was soon to become law.

V

King Takes Over

KING'S FIRST NIGHT in the Nueces Strip country was spent at the home of Doc White. The newcomer got a firsthand report of Mexican bandits that were operating from south of the Río Grande, preying upon livestock and engaging in other mischief. Indians, attacking from their Mexican bases, added to the constant peril in the Pendencia settlement. And King heard woeful tales about the influx of thieves and desperadoes who had gravitated to the border from the north, rounding up stray cattle, stealing from homesteaders, and hiding from the law—such as there was. These men were dubbed "G.T.T.'s" (gone to Texas) by their neighbors and officers who searched for them.

The new arrival on the Pendencia was promptly employed by the settlers to ride the ranges and protect the livestock that carried their brands. He pitched headlong into this challenging new enterprise and soon became a hard-riding, fearless crusader in behalf of those for whom he worked. His nature had yearned for just this sort of freedom and excitement. He enjoyed the responsibility of making his own decisions and planning his own strategy, and his natural yearning for leadership began to assert itself.

King heard tales about Cortina, the most daring and notorious of Mexican bandits, and he was soon clashing

28

with the Mexican chief's *bandidos* who stole, killed, and plundered on the American side of the Río Grande.

Everywhere King went in the chaparral he saw stray cattle and horses, some unbranded, waiting for takers. Cattle were selling for up to ten dollars a head if delivered to the drovers who were collecting for the big drives up the trail. There was also a lively market for horses, and Fisher was a lover of the untamed Spanish mustangs. His greatest thrill at that time was astride a wild cayuse with his spurs digging in.

It was during this period that King learned to shoot. There was plenty of room for practice, and there was a lot of time to spare. He developed a capacity for the quick draw, using either hand, or the two simultaneously. Not content to be second best, he practiced and brought the art to a state of perfection. Cool-headed, athletic, and precise, he could soon handle his pistols with the skill of a trained juggler. With him gunmanship seemed a natural gift.

King enjoyed the social life of the settlement. Sarah Vivian's charm had developed, and they were often seen together, riding horseback or dancing at neighborhood functions. Their devotion to each other was becoming quite apparent.

The King broke and trained the best horses obtainable. Irrepressible, he moved about in the shadows of night, chasing Mexican bandits across the river, often retrieving stolen horses and cattle to be returned to their owners on the Pendencia. The settlers soon developed a genuine respect and admiration for the youthful cowboy.

Fisher gave the name of "Yaller Lightnin' " to his favorite mount, which he had roped out of a bunch of mustangs. Under saddle it was said Old Yaller could "pace a mile a minute."

29

One day in a remote part of Zavala County he encountered a band of Mexican rustlers who were moving a herd of cattle toward the Río Grande [Leakey, *The West That Was*]. King met up with Joel Fenley and his son, George, who were also tracking the stolen cattle, and the three men joined forces.

In hot pursuit they soon overtook the stolen herd. It was noon, and the bandits were gathered around a campfire eating lunch. The pursuers, deciding to face the culprits, cautiously rode into their camp. There they announced their intention of cutting out certain brands which they owned. The Mexicans were content to stand by and allow the ranchmen to help themselves. George Fenley sat on his horse, at a good vantage point, with his rifle across his saddle bow, while his father and young King proceeded to retrieve their cattle, without incident.

Such acts of daring became commonplace, and King soon found himself surrounded by well-wishers and admirers—both good and bad. The worst of the border ruffians and cutthroats seemed to enjoy his company, and at the same time he was pleasantly received by the law-abiding element with whom he came in contact. His smooth, friendly, disarming nature made him a favorite everywhere he went. Thus, while yet in his teens, King found himself a leader among men.

Having achieved miracles in protecting the livestock of the Pendencia ranchmen, he decided it was time to begin his own brand. He located a ranch for himself in the community, built corrals, rounded up unbranded livestock, broke horses, and delivered longhorns to the drovers—a convenient source of income. He began to feel like a King, and he looked restlessly for new worlds to conquer.

As he dashed about, always leading the men he worked

with, displaying courage that bordered on rashness, the name "King Fisher" was becoming known in every saloon on the border, at cow camps, and on the range. His reputation as an expert horseman, gunslinger, and detective spread like wildfire up and down the border. No one wanted to tangle with him. The exercise and climate were agreeable, and the young man gained weight and maturity. His fine physique, his winning mannerisms, and his eagerness to lend a hand when action was required all set the stage for leadership and adoration.

Perhaps King's earliest weakness was in trusting those who seemed to trust him, without asking questions. It was not his nature to turn a man away who sought refuge at the Pendencia ranch. The criminal element soon learned they would not be reported to the law. Many of them had no place to hang their hats. They were on the loose, seeking shelter, free meals, and a chance to put their talents to use. Thousands of stray and unbranded cattle were in the Nueces Strip; and with a ready market waiting for the herds thus to be gathered, the King took many of the strangers in, asked no questions, and put them to work.

With this array of toughies, King had a formidable gang about him, all loyal, anxious, and willing to follow his commands. In an area infested with renegades and being invaded by Mexican *bandidos*, Fisher marshaled a superior force and laid the ground work for the building of an empire. Now respected and feared, the young man was prepared to consolidate his gains and capitalize upon the natural advantages afforded by an open, unprotected, and lawless area.

The gang that congregated at the Pendencia headquarters included many desperate men; but the King, evidently somewhat embittered by his brush with the law at Goliad,

31

seemed to feel he was operating in a desperate country where it was in order for him to make his own laws and choose his own associates.

It is considered likely that the crowd that operated out of Fisher's rendezvous in groups, often beyond the presence of their leader, and with many of them more or less, "on their own," may have engaged in acts of lawlessness which Fisher, had he known, would not have condoned. But he was tolerant toward the men, accepting at face value their versions of the many escapades that marked their movements in a wild and untamed country. They were loyal to King, and he meted out loyalty in return.

Unchallenged, he basked in the sunlight of prominence and unaccustomed adoration. As one writer put it, "King Fisher parlayed personality, gun skill, diplomacy and aggressiveness into a fabulous southwest Texas empire" [Holloway, *Texas Gun Lore*].

VI

Lawlessness in the Nueces Strip

ANY ATTEMPT TO APPRAISE King Fisher must be done against the backdrop of conditions prevailing along the Mexican border during the seventies. He became an integral part of the history that was being made there. An undeclared war was raging between Mexican outlaws who used Mexico as a sanctuary and the hard-bitten settlers who got in their way. And native outlaws were busy, living off the fat of the land, stealing, killing, and gambling. Ill will and bitter feeling had been mounting along the border ever since the Texas Revolution.

After the Battle of San Jacinto in 1836, Santa Anna agreed upon the Río Grande as the dividing line between Mexico and Texas. But the Mexican Congress refused to accept this division line. Thereafter, for a period of twelve years, the Mexicans disputed the boundary. This dispute was not settled until the Mexican War, which ended in the peace of Guadalupe Hidalgo in 1848. During this period Mexican military forces, in strength, made at least two major raids into San Antonio, one led by General Rafael Vasquez, and the other by the comic-opera French general, Adrian Woll. Smarting from these insults, the Texans tried to capture Santa Fe.

Also, by way of retaliation, three hundred hot-headed Texans took it upon themselves to march across the Río

Grande in an ill-fated invasion of their own. They engaged a large force of Mexicans at Mier and although they inflicted heavy casualties on the enemy, they were hopelessly outnumbered and finally surrendered.

The invaders were marched in chains, single file, from Mier to Monterrey, thence to Saltillo, and from there to Salado. In a break for freedom 193 of them escaped and then became lost in the desert, where for days they were without food or water. Most of the escapees were rounded up, and when they were returned to prison the infamous decimation was carried out—each blindfolded prisoner drawing a bean from a jar filled with 90 per cent white and 10 per cent black beans. The ones who drew the black ones were shot—and there were seventeen of them. Forty of the survivors died in the filth of Perote Prison in Mexico City, to which they were taken. Finally, the survivors were returned, via Tampico and New Orleans [see items by Green and Wade cited in bibliography].

News of the inhuman treatment accorded the captured Texans following their defeat at Mier spread through the country. Texans were determined to avenge these murders. Tempers flared. The incident added fuel to the conflict between the two countries and inflamed the minds of settlers who dared live along the border, from Brownsville to Eagle Pass. There was raiding and counter-raiding—an eye for an eye and a tooth for a tooth.

This state of mind and the attendant conflict continued long after the peace treaty of Guadalupe Hidalgo had been signed. While it was meaningful in international parlance, the treaty hardly served to abate the strife along the Mexican border.

Texas, burdened with a seven-million-dollar public debt and an unprotected border and frontier, was admitted to the Union in 1845. It had become increasingly difficult for the new Republic to support a government and protect its sprawling frontier. In admitting Texas, the federal government assumed responsibility for protecting its borders and its frontier.

But it was a long distance from Washington to the Quasado, and the protection that was supposed to come was either nonexistent or of little consequence. More than thirty years later—on January 2, 1879—Governor Richard Hubbard in a message to the state legislature on frontier problems reminded them of the failure of the federal government to meet its obligation. He said Texas had been compelled to spend over two million dollars in her own defense because of inaction from Washington.

The federal government did get around to building some forts along the Río Grande and along the sprawling western perimeter of settlements, then harassed by Indian incursions. Fort Brown was established at Brownsville, and farther up the river were built several other forts, including Ringgold Barracks, Fort Duncan, and Fort Clark.

Another line of forts dotted the western area of the state, from the Río Grande to the Red River. Along this line there was Fort McKavett, Fort Concho, Fort Griffin, and Fort Richardson, with Fort Sill next beyond the Red River. Fort Chadbourne in Coke County was built in 1852 to guard the Butterfield Overland Mail Route and add to the frontier protection complex. While the outposts were helpful, the great distances between these forts, as well as the use of green and inexperienced troops, served to limit their effectiveness in coping with border conditions that had long since become intolerable.

In the absence of adequate federal help, the state of Texas attempted to police some of the area by creating a Ranger force, headed for a time by the famous Captain John Coffee (Jack) Hays, who had directed a Ranger contingent during the days of the Republic.

A Ranger captain at the age of twenty-three, Hays served with such brilliance in ferreting out crime and repelling invading bandits and desperadoes, as well as Indians, that he more than any one created the early image of audacity and devotion to duty that has characterized the Texas Ranger in history and in legend for more than one hundred years.

Then came the Civil War, and for four long years the border was even less protected. This tragic turn of events played into the hands of the Mexican *bandidos*, who proceeded to take full advantage of the unguarded border between the countries.

The leader of the Mexican marauders was named Juan Nepomuceno Cortina. Born May 16, 1824, at Camargo, Tamaulipas, his twice-divorced mother was named Estefano. She was heiress to fabulous Spanish land grants around Brownsville. Cortina spent his early years on a rancho owned by his mother on the Texas side of the Río Grande near Brownsville.

For some twenty-five years Juan spearheaded a bloody conflict that kept the entire border area in an uproar.

In appearance Cortina was described as a *huero*, or red complexioned. A powerful man physically, this Spanish *grandee* of Castilian blood was cold blooded, bitterly anti-American, and a border terror. Known as "The Red Robber of the Río Grande," he became supreme commander of the largest band of cutthroats and thieves ever assembled in northern Mexico.

During General Zachary Taylor's invasion of Mexico, Juan served as a spy and guerilla in the Mexican forces, and was rewarded with a lieutenant's commission. After the war he was dismissed from the army when he was caught stealing horses belonging to his own government. The next year he murdered his employer.

At San José, Juan's mother's hacienda above Brownsville, which Juan converted into a military camp, supported by some four hundred or five hundred armed followers, the brash bandit leader emitted his hatred for the gringos by issuing a proclamation, reading:

> Our purpose has been to punish the infamous villainy of our enemies. They have banded together . . . to pursue and rob us for no other reason except that we are by birth Mexicans. . . . An organized society of Mexicans in the State of Texas will untiringly devote itself to the extermination of their tyrants until its philanthropic purpose of bettering the condition of the unfortunate Mexicans who reside here shall have been attained.

Elusive and insolent, Cortina ruled over the bandits and other criminals in much of northern Mexico with an iron fist. We think today of Pancho Villa as Mexico's leading villain on the border. But he could hardly have held a light for his predecessor who terrorized the Río Grande a half century before him.

A contributing cause of the smuggling which was carried on along the border during Cortina's reign was a strip of country known as *Zona Libre*, or Free Zone, which stretched six to eight miles wide and extended northward from the Gulf for more than five hundred miles up the Río Grande on the Mexican side.

The *Zona Libre* fit into the pattern of the Cortina operations. The Mexican chieftain proceeded to license his raiders, paying them fifty cents a head for stolen cattle brought into the zone. He took what he termed his "royal fifth," taking every fifth animal as a "pecho" tax, thus implementing the *Zona Libre* with his own devices.

Cortina's grandmother was named Nanita. And Juan proceeded to lay claim to all cattle along the border, contending they had descended from Nanita's brand and therefore were his by right of inheritance. In addition, he maintained that all land lying between the Nueces and the Río Grande belonged to Mexico. He flew the Mexican flag on Texas soil. He is believed to have had three thousand organized and licensed raiders, assigned to the stealing of livestock on the American side. He maintained twenty large ranch spreads facing the Río Grande where cattle were collected in preparation for sale in Cuban markets. It is said that by systematic stealing his *muchachos* drove enough cattle across the Río Grande to stock his four favorite ranches—the Canela, the Soldadito, the Caritas, and the Palito Blanco—with cattle left over to sell in Cuba.

On the Texas side these ruffians were stampeding their way through the thickets and the cactus, snatching Nanita's cattle from the unguarded ranges, then collecting their bounty when they were delivered on the other side. Juan informed his thieves that if they stole in Mexico they would be hanged, but he would look out for them when they brought cattle across from Texas. Operating in armed bands, these outlaws gathered as many as five hundred stolen cattle at one time. In one instance there were eighty *Cortinistas* driving one herd. Historians estimated that the Mexicans stole as many as 900,000 head of cattle on the Texas side [Dobie, Pate, Webb, and Wantland].

At the end of the Civil War the U.S. government gave but scant attention to the border troubles. Sparsely settled, the country that comprised the Nueces Strip was the focal point of continued turmoil and trouble. The Nueces River had already gained the description of "the Sheriff's deadline." Beyond it murder, stealing, and all forms of lawlessness prevailed in abundance. The triangle comprising the Strip was some three hundred miles long and from one hundred to two hundred miles in width. At the end of the War and for a few years following, it was estimated about 80 per cent of the population were Mexican. Some of these were loyal and law abiding, but the patriotic feelings of many of them were divided.

The problem on the Texas side was aggravated by a growing resentment against the prosperity of so-called cattle barons. Despite setbacks and hardships, these intrepid ranchmen managed to prosper and expand. They found themselves beset not only by invading *ladrones* but also by an influx of domestic thieves.

This condition of crime and lawlessness continued up through the mid-1870's. A study of border conditions reveals that trouble with the Mexicans was probably at its worst from 1871 to 1875. It was during this four-year period that raids were made with most regularity. As late as March, 1875, 150 Mexican bandits were reported crossing the river near Eagle Pass. The crossing party then separated into four groups, and then they set out on plunder binges. One of the groups was intercepted by the U.S. Army.

Throughout the seventies this wholesale stealing continued, although the law gained the upper hand by the middle of that decade. And stealing was by no means confined to cattle. In a period of three years, from 1875 to 1878, it was estimated that no fewer than 100,000 horses were stolen in the same area that cattle stealing was occurring.

When demand for beef dropped, the rustlers continued stealing cattle because of the ready market for hides and tallow. Throughout the chaparral thousands of carcasses were left for coyotes and javelinas to devour, and bleached bones littered the countryside—the Skinning War, it was called. In 1872, 300,000 hides were shipped from Corpus Christi and Rockport. Tallow and hides moved by ox carts from the range to the markets, on either side of the border. The Texas cattle that were stolen by the *Cortinistas* were often sold in Mexico for one-fifth of what their owners could have received on the American side, whether sold for hides and tallow or for beef.

Before the advent of the Rangers, in many areas there was only token law enforcement. In some counties no one would apply for the job of sheriff.

Ranger Captain L. H. McNelly underscored the conditions in testimony given to the U.S. Claims Commission in 1872:

> Many of them [border citizens] have not nerve enough to take an active, decided stand, either by giving information or by personal assistance. Still, a number of them have done it since I have been out there, and some eight or ten, probably twelve, have been killed on that account. It has been the history of these border counties that when any man, Mexican or American, has made himself prominent in hunting these raiders down, or in organizing parties to pursue them when they are carrying off cattle, he has been either forced to move from the ranch and come into town or he has been killed. . . . While the resident Mexican population who have any property are in sympathy with our people, there is a large floating population who have come over from the other side . . . and who are spies and informers of the raiders.

Finally, there were some crossings in "hot pursuit." General Ronald S. MacKenzie, with eleven troops of cavalry, crossed the river near Del Río, penetrating 150 miles. The Secretary of War had sent orders to General E. O. S. Ord, commander of the Department of Texas, dated June 1, 1877, which left no doubt concerning the ticklish authority to cross the international border:

In case the lawless invasions continue, you will be at liberty . . . when in pursuit of marauders, and when your troops are in sight of them or upon a fresh trail, to follow them across the Río Grande and to overtake and punish them and retake property stolen from the United States citizens on the other side of the line.

A number of crossings were made after that, all in "hot pursuit" of bandits, and some of the pursuits were quite effective. Much of this relentless war against the thieves, both Mexican and Indian, was waged under the command of Lieutenant John Bullis.

After a decade of virtual anarchy the outlook for some assistance on the Mexican side was brightened by the ascendancy to power of the revolutionary leader, Porfirio Díaz. The latter took over the government in 1876, calling immediately upon Generals Canales and Geronimo Trevino, who commanded along the border, to enforce the law, prevent raids, and co-operate with U.S. authorities. The United States recognized the Díaz government in April, 1878.

But King Fisher had entered the maelstrom in 1871, when conditions were at their worst and law enforcement was practically nonexistent. His move to the Pendencia was in the midst of the disreputable reconstruction. And the fortunes of fate, perhaps more than premeditated design, maneuvered the seventeen-year-old-King into the camp of the trouble makers and caused his subsequent ascendancy to power and control.

VII

King's Escapades

THE TOWN OF EAGLE PASS, on the surface as lazy and contented as a milch cow, was a dot on the map when the 1870's came along. As county seat, it attracted settlers from the hinterlands who came to record their deeds and cattle brands, stock up on pinto beans and sourdough ingredients, and pick up the latest border gossip. The chances were that any gossip would feature the hottest news then making the rounds—King Fisher. Early in the decade Eagle Pass became King Fisher's town.

Gamblers and would-be thieves visited the trading post from time to time, patronizing the saloons and gambling places and checking on their status and security. As the decade advanced this border town became a port of entry to Mexico, and its trade territory extended to both sides of the river. The Spaniards had called it *Paso de Aguila* because of the vast number of Mexican eagles that migrated across the Río Grande at this point. First settled in 1849, on the heels of the Mexican War, during which a temporary military encampment sprang up, the newly populated community was called Camp Eagle Pass. Fort Duncan, built just above the town in 1850, helped form the nucleus of the small settlement that followed. In keeping with the times, the first business at Eagle Pass is said to have been a saloon, installed by Henry Matson in a borrowed tent. Emigrants headed for El Paso, New Mexico, and California came this way, and a stagecoach connected the town with San Antonio as early as 1851. It was the western border anchor of the Nueces Strip and was soon to become the nerve center of King Fisher Territory.

West of Eagle Pass there was some livestock activity as far as San Felipe and the Devil's River.

Many of the early settlers in the town were Latin-Americans. Trinidad San Miguel, a highly respected citizen of Eagle Pass for more than half a century, was one of the seventy, with their families, who went there from San Antonio when the fort was opened.

"Trinny," as San Miguel was called, who passed away in 1938 at the age of seventy-nine, had been a close friend and admirer of King Fisher's. He also prized his friendship with former Vice-President John Nance Garner and the late Congressman Milton West, of Brownsville. Throughout his life San Miguel was quick to defend Fisher's name when it came under criticism. He had served as tax collector and had held other offices in Maverick County for many years.

His surviving son, Refugio, now living in Eagle Pass, recently recalled some of the episodes of the King, as recounted to him by his late father.

"One time my mother purchased a Spanish pony from the other side of the river," he said. "It disappeared, and it was believed some of King Fisher's men had taken it in their roundups. My mother was very unhappy about this loss because she valued the horse very highly. My father took this up with King, described the horse, and asked him to help locate it. The very next day the horse was returned to our house."

Another incident recalled by Refugio concerned a time when two of Fisher's men made a wager about their marksmanship. It happened on a hot day in Eagle Pass. Full of mischief and with nothing better to do, the two men cast their eyes at one Prajedes, a wood hauler, driving his ox cart lazily down the street. One said to the other, "I'll take the brindle ox and you take the other. If I fail to kill mine, I'll give you $15. If you miss, you give me $15."

"It's a bet," and in a flash the two drew and fired their pistols simultaneously, and both oxen fell dead in the middle of Main Street, right in front of what is now the Eagle Pass Drug Store.

Prajedes, fearing the next shot might be aimed at him, lost no time in leaving his team to their fate. He disappeared in the direction of his adobe hut. A few minutes later King came along, saw the dead oxen, and asked Trinidad, who was surveying the incident, who killed them. When he learned what had happened, the King told Trinny to take him to see the owner.

As they approached Prajedes' home they were met by the *Señora*, who insisted nervously that her husband was not at home. Trinny convinced her they were there to help, not to harm, them. They were then admitted, and she motioned to Trinidad to look under the bed. There they found Prajedes. They persuaded him to come out and then asked him about the damages. The Mexican said twenty-five dollars would be enough. The two visitors then returned to town, and Fisher demanded an explanation of the two pranksters. When they related to him how it all happened, Fisher told them that since the oxen were killed simultaneously, it was a draw, that they both lost the bet and each therefore owed fifteen dollars. He collected the thirty dollars and took it to Prajedes, who was well pleased with the settlement [see the work by Florence Kellogg].

"My father always said King Fisher was a 'muy bueno

hombre,' and that regardless of what was said about him, he meant well," concluded Refugio.

There were several saloons in Eagle Pass at the time. One, the "Old Blue Saloon," owned by John Vivian, was often frequented by King who, however, was not given to drinking liquor to excess. In fact, later, Fisher himself owned an interest in a saloon, probably the "Old Blue."

As a young ranchman, there was never a dull moment for the King. With flashy dress and a polished bearing, he was accepted in all circles among the local people. He had a way of dispelling the uneasiness that was often felt when he entered the company of those who knew him only by reputation.

E. H. Schmidt, a prominent Eagle Pass banker, recalls that his mother, a contemporary of Fisher's, told of the times when the handsome cowboy would ride into Eagle Pass when community dances were held. "He danced with every woman present, according to my mother. He was very popular and acted the part of a perfect gentleman," she said.

He also appeared at community dances in Uvalde. F. W. Pulliam, a pioneer Crystal City ranchman, remembers his late mother's telling of her acquaintance with the King. She told of how the visitor danced with her and others and said "he always behaved like a perfect gentleman."

Once when King was on a train a man who was drinking became rude to two Catholic nuns. Fisher immediately interceded and put a stop to the man's fun. Several days later the nuns met their benefactor on the streets of Eagle Pass and expressed their appreciation [Kellogg].

King's widow described the King as unusually handsome, tall and black-headed, with one brown and one black eye. She said he always wore the most excellent black broadcloth suits and the best white shirts that he could buy. He

45

sported big white sombreros and black patent leather boots, with intricate trimmings. Most of his clothes were purchased in Ciudad P. Díaz, across the river, now known as Piedras Negras [Kellogg].

Before Porfirio Díaz, the revolutionary leader, ascended to power, Díaz was well known along the border. In fact, much of his planning that led to the overthrow of the Mexican regime took place in Brownsville. For two or three years before becoming President in 1876, Díaz lived part of the time at Piedras Negras.

During that time he and King Fisher became good friends. On occasions, King's widow recalled, General Díaz invited King and Sarah to be his guests at balls and receptions. The General always sent a bodyguard to escort them over, a necessity because many Mexicans had threatened to kill Fisher if they ever caught him in Mexico. Díaz presented King with a beautiful pistol on one occasion.

Díaz, in his struggle for power, cultivated the good will and support of many Americans along the border, and King was the object of many of his courtesies and overtures. At the same time Díaz numbered among his good friends on the Texas side of the river such men as John (Old Rip) Ford in the Brownsville area.

The late W. A. Bonnet met Fisher when Bonnet moved to Eagle Pass in 1878. He got to know the King well and often visited with him.

"When I came to Eagle Pass as a boy in 1878," he later recalled, "King Fisher was very well known around here for not standing for any foolishness. Some called him a desperado, but I do not think him as bad as pictured.

"I once asked King how many men he had killed and he said: 'Seven.' I said I thought it was more than that. He replied: 'Oh, I don't count Mexicans!' " [Bonnet].

Judge Bonnet wrote about an occasion when the border leader's men came to town, celebrating, and in keeping with custom proceeded to do some shooting around town.

He reported that Judge Stone fined them and they became angered, contending they were only having a good time. Later that day while they were riding around a brush fence and through a mesquite thicket (now the center of business of Main Street in Eagle Pass) some Mexican friends of the Judge shot and killed two, wounding the third. The two were buried on the spot, and the third was taken to a house two blocks away where he died later. The skeletons of these two, according to Bonnet, were found some fifty years later when an excavation was being made for the Aztec Theater.

Continuing to reminisce, Bonnet added: "Please do not think from what I have said that King Fisher was a bad man, as men were here then. There were many like him, only worse. It took men like this to make the frontier fit for us to live in today."

Bonnet worked in a store, across the street from a saloon. He recalled a fight at the saloon. There was shooting, and Fisher emerged. "I thought you liked a fight," Bonnet commented to the King. "I never fight unless I have to," replied Fisher, which, according to Bonnet, was probably true.

Another Eagle Pass resident recently recalled: "I remember my grandmother telling of the times when King Fisher would come to town with his crowd, whooping it up. They would sometimes shoot out the street lights, but Fisher would come back the next day and pay for all the damages his men had caused."

One time, early in his career, King tangled with a soldier at a social function. Fisher's conduct offended the commanding officer. The latter ordered his cavalrymen to capture the elusive visitor who had made a hasty exit. Later King told the Doc Whites about how he outwitted the pursuers by concealing himself in a thick growth, dismounting and stroking his horse's nose to prevent him from neighing—one of his horse's habits when other horses approached.

In later years, the King's widow recalled another experience involving Fisher and Trinidad San Miguel. The latter had acquired a fine gray horse but had neglected to put his brand on him. Picked up by some of Fisher's men, the horse was taken to the ranch, and Fisher put a brand on it. When Trinny missed his horse, he went to the justice of the peace, who told him he had heard King Fisher had the horse, and that if he wanted a gray horse he would be well advised to go buy one and forget about the other. But Trinidad knew better. When he saw the King he told him about losing the gray horse. "Is that your horse?" Fisher asked. Upon being assured it was, Fisher went with San Miguel to the ranch, and the owner soon returned to town leading the animal.

Another story, which serves to illustrate the King's interest in the unfortunate, concerns a poor Mexican who put his brand on a maverick which was claimed by an Anglo. It was not uncommon for ranchmen to brand mavericks, but the Mexican was hailed into court. He came in, followed by two small children. It happened that King Fisher was in the room at the time, and he asked where the children's mother was. The Mexican replied that she was dead and that he had no one with whom to leave the children. Fisher then intervened and convinced the judge that the Mexican needed to care for the children more than the state needed him in the penitentiary, and the defendant was promptly freed.

Admirers of the King were varied and numerous. One of them was John Leakey, who as a young man knew the border character.

> King was a handsome man with black eyes and black hair and mustache, noted for his fine bearing and appearance as he rode through the towns and bottoms of southwest Texas, followed by his flashy vaqueros. He always rode beautiful horses and dressed well. To me, an eleven-year-old boy, it was a black day when King Fisher, in the prime of his life, was cut down by an assassin's bullet in San Antonio [Leakey].

Frank Bushick, editor of the *San Antonio Express* from 1892 to 1906, recorded the impressions he had gained of the notorious King. He wrote that Mexican bandits had been driving off cattle and the gringo boys thought it proper to play even. He told of some dealings Fisher once had with a man named Donophan, who operated a cattle ranch a few miles below Eagle Pass during the time that King Fisher held forth on the Pendencia, some thirty miles away. According to this source, ill feeling developed between the two groups, and Donophan accused the Fisher crowd of killing some of the cattle belonging to Donophan and an associate named Porter. It was not long until one or more killings were committed by each side.

Another incident concerned C. S. Brodbent, who operated a small sheep ranch between the Donophan range and the Pendencia. On a Sunday morning Brodbent started out with his herd, grazing them over the hills to a pond of water where he maintained a range camp. As he approached the water, a Mexican suddenly appeared out of the brush, and Brodbent also saw a bunch of horses grazing a half mile away.

The Mexican told Brodbent that he was camped at the

water hole with some other men, and they turned out to be King Fisher's men. The Mexican also said they were short on food and would like to buy two of his sheep, and the sheepherder acceded. Two of the half dozen men at the camp shot two of the sheep. Each of Fisher's men was armed with a Winchester, a pistol, knife, and two cartridge belts.

As Fisher's men dressed the sheep and were cooking some of it, the King himself rode up. "Is that your camp down the valley?" he asked Brodbent. Being told it was, Fisher said to him: "We've been down there and baked a couple of pones of bread, and I'll pay for 'em. We were hungry."

The sheepman refused pay, but at Fisher's invitation he joined the party for dinner, all hunkering down cowboy style as they ate from the roast mutton and cornbread, which they all seemed to enjoy.

King's men seemed hungry for news about themselves. They asked Brodbent if he had any newspapers, but when the sheepman produced some religious papers that had been sent to him by Baptist friends in Philadelphia, one of them snapped: "Oh, hell, this is a damned religious paper," and handed it back.

They then asked if Brodbent had seen anything of the Porter outfit. Only a day or two earlier the sheep raiser had seen the Porters, who had asked questions about Fisher's outfit. This indicated to Brodbent that trouble was brewing, and he kept quiet.

After an hour of talk and rest in the moat of trees that surrounded the water hole, Brodbent left to tend his sheep. That night the Donophan ranch house was burned—by whom no one seemed to know.

A few evenings later Donophan rode into Brodbent's

camp and spent the night. He told Brodbent he had found two of his cattle shot, and be believed it was done by the King Fisher gang. He decided to ride down toward the Pendencia and see about it. The sheepman cautioned him about the danger of going there, particularly alone. The reply was, "I'm not afraid of them; if they shoot me they'll have to be mighty quick about it." His friend replied: "Well, if they want to kill you they will not be very ceremonious about it."

The next day Donophan departed—toward the Pendencia country. He was never seen alive again by any friend. Who was responsible for his death and under what circumstances he died became subjects of conjecture. Whether the King knew about it could never be determined. He had some dangerous characters in his outfit, and he was not always around when they did their dirty work. The tragedy was regarded as another blow in the feudal war then raging [Bushick, *Glamorous Days*].

There were several other hearsay reports of clashes in the chaparral, involving Fisher and his men. Several years later Major T. T. Teel, a noted criminal lawyer, who later represented King on several occasions in court, told of how the Pendencia ranchman once interrupted several Mexicans who were removing a horse from Fisher's corral. The horse was claimed by the Mexicans, but when one of them fired at Fisher, according to Teel, the King pounced like a panther upon his assailant, took the gun away from him, and killed three of them with it. He was indicted for this, and Teel served as his attorney [*San Antonio Express*, March 13, 1884].

Teel also told of a time when some Mexicans allegedly stole a bunch of ninety cattle in Mexico and sold them to Fisher, giving him a bill of sale. Alejo Gonzales, the owner of the cattle, followed the trail of the rustlers, tracking them

51

to King's pasture. The Mexican owner and his men started to drive the recovered cattle back to Mexico, along with a number of King's cattle that bore his brand and mixed with the cattle claimed by Gonzales.

When Fisher learned of this he summoned a few of his gang and followed and overtook Gonzales. A gun battle ensued, with Fisher doing the shooting on his side, according to the attorney. Three Mexicans were killed by Fisher during the battle, and another was wounded.

Teel, a member of the law firm of Merchant, Teel & Wilcox, of San Antonio, was rated high as a criminal lawyer. He was always on hand when court met in Uvalde and Eagle Pass. Even before the Civil War he had a large practice in and around San Antonio. He, like many of his contemporaries, had a weakness for gambling, and was hauled into court a few times when raids on gambling halls were made. He was fined ten dollars for betting at Uvalde in May, 1874. But in those days such charges did little to detract from a man's reputation. Receiving such a fine was a lot like getting a traffic ticket today.

In later life Teel moved to El Paso, where he was living at the time of his death. The late Robert T. Neill, of San Angelo, knew Teel when the two practiced law in El Paso. "Out there he kind of played out in his old age," recalled Neill. "He was a friend of my father's, who knew him in San Antonio. I talked with him the night before he died."

Tom Sullivan was brought to Texas before the Civil War by his master, Bill Redus. A 1935 story in the *Fort Worth Press* told of an interview with old Tom. The former slave became deputy sheriff of Medina County after he was granted his freedom. Later he was constable to John Regas, when the latter was justice of the peace. It was while he was an officer that he brought drinks and cigars to King Fisher, who was in the Castroville jail for having pursued some Mexican cattle thieves across the Río Grande and killed them. He had brought back their remains, according to Sullivan. Tom also knew Ben Thompson and was quite friendly with him.

A *Frontier Times* article (November, 1949) quoted Sullivan as saying: "They called King Fisher and Ben Thompson bad men, but they wasn't bad men; they just wouldn't stand for no foolishness, and they never killed any one unless they bothered them."

Continuing, Sullivan said: "King Fisher lived in a hole in the Nueces River Bank for a month before he was caught."

This cave dwelling dovetails with another story recorded by John Leakey, told to the latter by King's most trusted employee—Pancho.

He [Pancho] told me that he and Fisher had a cave on the Nueces River where they used to hide out. The cave was located between the old 7D ranch headquarters and Evans Lake, in the second bank of the river. I have been there myself, and I saw King's and Pancho's names carved inside. There was another name, too, Pablo. He was one of the vaqueros King killed, later.

It was as pretty a place as you ever walked into, and well chosen for secrecy. As late as 1913 I was in that cave, and I noticed some old, dusty, sealed buckets and an old lantern. I looked into the buckets. They were full of beans and coffee. On account of the dryness in the cave the buckets hadn't rusted inside and the beans and coffee were good. I didn't think much about it then, except for the surprise that the stuff was in such good condition, but I think now what valuable old relics those old buckets would be.

Leakey then repeated Pancho's story, as told to Leakey, about the time that some of King's Mexican employees brought cattle in from the range or from Mexico, and the animals were being branded and sold off. Pancho told of Pablo's demise at the hands of King. Pablo was only one of the four who were killed that day. The four men were branding in the pens north of the old 7D, and the Mexicans were grumbling about how the cattle were being divided.

Fisher assured them that their full share would be made up out of the next bunch they brought in, but that did not satisfy them.

King saw they were planning to kill him. He didn't let on. He went right on branding, and watching. Out to one side Pancho was tending the branding irons. One Mexican was working with King, three sat on the fence. King always wore his six-shooter, according to Pablo's version; therefore the men, who had too often seen the results of Fisher's aim, were not anxious to start anything.

One of the three men on the fence wore a gun, too, and he was the one King watched the closest. But it was the one helping with the branding who started the argument, and then tried to put up a fight. King saw his first move, and brained him with a branding iron. In a flash the armed Mexican jumped into the pen, his hand on his gun. King drew and shot him before he could draw the gun, then whirled and killed the two on the fence.

Pancho deplored the killings but said nothing—just helped King dig the graves and bury the dead. Later he put up markers at the graves [Durham, *Taming the Nueces Strip*].

Pancho told Leakey they didn't use the cave because of

54

the killings—that nobody bothered about that—but because of the cattle they brought in from other parts of the country. He said King ranged from the Nueces to the Chicon, and all the way from Eagle Pass to Carrizo Springs, and as far down as Brudin Lake on the Nueces below Cotulla, which Pancho said was where the cattle came from.

Pancho mentioned the rumor that there were eight—not four—killed in that fight, but insisted that in reality there were only four.

The rumor that King had killed eight Mexicans, persisted, however, and was repeated by Ranger George Durham.

"It is said," he wrote, "with how much truth cannot be asserted, that King Fisher killed near Espantosa Lake, in Dimmit County, eight Mexicans who had just delivered to him a herd of 'wet cattle' and with whom he had quarreled over the price. King Fisher had a definitive way of settling quarrels. . . ." [Durham].

As a further illustration of how the rumors of the King's exploits got mixed up, and the many versions distorted, Ranger N. A. Jennings, apparently referring to the same killing, wrote:

"A few weeks before we arrested them, King Fisher and Frank Porter, by themselves, rode around the herd and killed every one of the eight Mexicans. The vaqueros were buried all together, and the place where they were buried was known as 'Frank Porter's Graveyard' " [Jennings, *A Texas Ranger*].

Jennings, described by Durham as "more of a writer than a Ranger," probably accepted the first version of the corral fight that was related to him. All indications are that these various stories concerned the same incident—each embellished or garbled in a different way. If any are to be accepted, it has to be Pancho's version. He was present and said there were four victims, and he alone among those who related the story of the shooting was in a position to know.

Major Teel, King's attorney, was quoted as saying, after the border leader's death, that "he was far from being the dangerous and unscrupulous desperado he is represented" [*San Antonio Express*, March 13, 1884]. He described Fisher's ranch as the headquarters for renegades and cattle thieves who had been outlawed and said Fisher always treated them well and fed them for their services on his ranch, and "he did not participate in their reckless lawlessness, but was generally credited with being their leader."

Another encounter between the King and the Mexican *bandidos* across the river was related by Judge N. A. Bonnet, citing "Pest House Pete," an old-time Eagle Pass fixture as his authority [Bonnet]. After Fisher's death, Pete (who got the sobriquet by having lived in an old pest house) told of many escapades which he claimed happened in earlier days when he worked for Fisher, but he always added, "Me no do nothing."

He told of a time when Fisher lived on the Nueces. After a hot pursuit of a band of invaders from Mexico he overtook and killed three of them on the other side of the river, then ordered Pete to fasten his rope to each of them and drag them back to the Texas side. And the same authority told of another fight on the Latin side of the river when Fisher got the better of it, killing one, and again told Pete to drag the victim back across the river.

Such stories may or may not be well founded. Anyone who knew King could recall reports of something he had done during his fantastic career, and it is to be expected that many of the tales were exaggerated, and, with repetition, became more frightening. And yet it is quite likely that the most hair-curling of incidents went unreported.

Judge Bonnet came up with still another episode. He told of a Seminole government guide who came into the Old Blue Saloon and ordered a drink. When asked to pay he became furious and began shooting. Indians were notorious for their inability to handle liquor. When it was all over, King Fisher had suffered a scalp wound, and the Seminole was wounded in the stomach. "It all happened so quick that no one could tell how it had happened," said Bonnet, who was working across the street from the saloon.

A secondhand appraisal of the notorious Fisher was given by John Leakey. The King employed Mexican workers on the old 7D ranch, one of them having been Pancho, his faithful worker. For years Pancho had accompanied Fisher on his rounds. He was an accomplished vaquero and was devoted to his boss, whom he later described as a "*muy buena hombre, muy buena corazon*"—a very good man, a good heart. Leakey added that Pancho probably knew Fisher better and knew more about him than any man who ever rode the range with him. He rode with him day and night, watching for signs of trouble, warning his *compadre* of danger when he saw it.

Teel, the lawyer, enjoying the confidential relationship of attorney and client, probably knew more about the King than most of his contemporaries. Referring to a murder case against Fisher, Teel said the charge was for killing a man named Donovan. "But he did not," the barrister insisted, "the proof showing that he knew of it but had no hand in the act."

"He shot a nigger full of bullets but did not kill him," Teel added.

The Rangers, he said, frequently told Fisher that if he and Wes Bruton would leave the country they would be permitted to go in peace, but they declined.

"At that time the country was full of cattle and horse thieves, and Fisher got credit of doing most of the stealing and killing from the fact that he was known to associate with thieves and harbored them at his home. Almost every killing or theft which occurred in that section was attributed to him or Bruton," the attorney related.

The King numbered among his close personal friends John Robert Baylor, who lived for a time in San Antonio and later at Montell in Uvalde County, where he engaged in ranching. Baylor died in 1894.

Baylor, a colorful frontiersman, had come to Texas from Kentucky, and he served in the Texas legislature in 1853, later as an agent to the Comanche Indians, and then as a colonel in the Confederate forces. In charge of the Texas Mounted Rifles, he was sent to El Paso, where he drove the Union forces out, and then served briefly as governor of Arizona.

Baylor once accompanied King to Laredo, where he assisted him in being cleared of what appeared to be false charges. Both Baylor and his son, George, visited with Fisher on occasions, and they appeared to enjoy each other's company.

The Montell ranchman's grandson, George W. Baylor, now of Tucson, recently recalled hearing his father tell firsthand stories of King's exploits, once saying to his son: "Anything that was done in that part of the country (and no witnesses), people would say, 'King Fisher must have done it.' "

George Baylor continued:

With a reputation which John R. Baylor had for fighting all his life for law and order, against Indians and paleface renegades, it is hard to believe that he would have been a friend of King Fisher if these legends had any truth to them. Yet I know that he as well as my father were staunch friends of his, not only as long as he lived, but as long as *they* lived.

After King was killed in 1884, he having been a candidate for sheriff of Uvalde County at the time, Henry W. Baylor entered the race, won, and was elected ten more times in succession. "The Baylors were backing King Fisher," recalls George Baylor, in a letter to the author, "and since he was killed they decided to put Henry in the race."

VIII

The King in Court

BY THE MID-SEVENTIES, when the law finally came to the chaparral, Fisher's reputation as a marksman had long been established. His name was synonymous with resolute courage, reckless daring, and dogged tenacity. In the far-flung border country, from Laredo to Eagle Pass, the King was not to be taken lightly. Being at odds with him was shunned by those who wanted to get along and live in the Strip.

Already the *Zona Libre* and the Nueces Strip existed, but now a new and meaningful description of the heart of the upper border country came into common parlance— "King Fisher's Territory." The Territory's borders were not delineated on the map, but everyone who lived within its confines was quite aware he was there through the sufferance of one man—King Fisher. His influence extended from the chaparral to the courthouses. His word was law throughout the Territory, comprising three or four counties, which some called the King's country. At his Pendencia headquarters upwards of one hundred men came and went, beholden to the chieftain.

Cattle business was good in the Strip during the seventies, with a lively market most of the time. The range was open, with no fences, and the unclaimed cattle which abounded during the Civil War, with their offspring, were numerous, though reduced by Cortina's henchmen and local thieves.

These longhorns had been found grazing in the brush by the earliest settlers. Their origin is a matter of conjecture. The more likely explanation is that they were descended from Spanish stock imported into Mexico by Hernando Cortes, the Conqueror, who had entered Mexico City in 1519. Wayne Gard, in his *The Chisholm Trail*, surmised these animals were driven across the Río Grande to be used by *vaqueros* for meat or as draft animals for the military expeditions and for use by mission settlements on the Texas side.

The mustangs, which were found in abundance by the first Anglo arrivals, were, according to Bard, from the Arab horses of northern Africa taken into Spain during the Moorish invasion, then brought to Mexico by Cortes along with the cattle.

As early as 1866 these Texas cattle began to move in great herds northward to Abilene, Dodge City, Cheyenne, and Santa Fe. In 1871 more than 700,000 longhorns went from Texas to Kansas. But the next year saw a slump in the market, followed by panic in 1873, when most of the Kansas City banks folded, and cattle sold in that market for as low as two and one-half cents a pound. In 1874 only 166,000 cattle were trailed, and the following year the number dropped to only 152,000.

The economic well-being of the settlers in the Nueces Strip went up and down, like the mercury in a thermometer, with the cattle markets, for the border country was essentially a one-crop economy—cattle.

By 1875 the Texas drovers had found a new market for their cattle, and the demand boomed. Previously the trailed cattle had been shipped from Kansas to the Atlantic seaboard. But a new market was opened with the demand for cattle to stock the vast grazing areas of the west, and Dodge

City was cowboy capital for a year or two, as large droves of longhorns were routed there, with others veering off to Cheyenne, Abilene, and other focal points and staging spots where they were received and sent on their way to new homes on the western range [Bard, Richardson, Nordyke, and Sandoz].

Market centers at the end of the trails were lush with money, and gamblers and those looking for easy money were attracted to the roaring frontier sites. It was only natural that the gunslingers were in demand, either for excitement, gambling, peace officers, or as professional fighting men for the great cattle outfits. King Fisher was reported to have been seen at Dodge City in 1877, and it is quite likely that he made more than one trip up the trail [Lake, *Wyatt Earp*].

As would be expected, King Fisher was to face charges in the courthouses. Having spent four months in prison when a boy, he wanted no more of that. He courted the friendship of officers, scanned the jury lists, and kept a wary eye on court proceedings.

The court records of Maverick County are replete with evidence indicating the influence once exerted by the King at the seat of justice. Back in 1872, only one year after Fisher had arrived on the Pendencia, when district court was by law scheduled to be in regular session on March 4, a notation on the docket states: "District Attorney was ill." Court minutes, noted by the clerk, stated that neither the judge nor the prosecutor showed up the next day; court then adjourned, with no business transacted.

While Fisher's influence may have had nothing to do with this strange occurrence, it is considered likely that his weight was already being manifested, particularly in view of later developments. Although then only eighteen years of age, his power and control were being felt in the sensitive business of meteing out justice in King Fisher Territory.

The next term of court was scheduled for the first Monday in July, 1872. Again neither judge nor prosecutor appeared. The judge who failed to show was J. J. Thornton, of the 24th Judicial District, and the district attorney at the time was T. M. Paschal.

This unexplained absence for two terms in succession was certainly not owing to lack of business that needed attention.

When November, 1872, came around, there was still evidence of difficulty in the court. The clerk's notation on the docket recited, "His honor Judge J. J. Thornton not having arrived, court adjourned until the next day." And again the next day, "His honor the Judge not yet having appeared, adjourned till next day."

But at eight o'clock that evening, according to docket notations, the situation had suddenly changed. "The court having arrived since the last entry above it is ordered that the court open pursuant to adjournment. Present: The Hon. George H. Noonan, Judge of the 73rd Judicial District, holding by interchange with the Hon. J. J. Thornton, Judge of the 24th Judicial District; Thomas M. Paschal, District Attorney, James A. Sumpter, Sheriff; Albert Turpe, Clerk."

Judge Noonan proceeded to empanel a grand jury, which included several who were known friends of the King— among them being George Carter, Charles H. Vivian, F. Zertuche, and others. Several indictments were returned. A murder case against one Williams was tried, and he was acquitted. Several other cases were disposed of, but the records are silent on King.

In those days the courts met three times each year, and the judges traveled from one county to another in their judicial districts. It is interesting to follow the court sessions at Eagle Pass during that period when many people preferred to make and administer their own law, unhampered by the meddling of courts.

At the next session that met, March 3, 1873, Judge Thornton was back on the bench after missing three sessions, and the district attorney was now A. A. Dial, who, incidentally, was later King Fisher's attorney. There were several indictments, but nothing noteworthy took place. The same was true when the court met again on December 1, 1873, having skipped one session.

There appears to have been no spring term in 1874, though one was scheduled as a matter of law. And again on August 3 of that year, the date fixed for a court session, the court met but transacted practically no business.

When court convened at Eagle Pass on December 7, 1874, the King's influence continued to be felt. The grand jury empaneled included King Fisher, along with P. B. Vivian, LaFayette Vivian, John Vivian (King's future father-in-law), and Charles Vivian. The young border leader had just celebrated his twenty-first birthday, and this was his first jury duty.

Four indictments were filed by the grand jury of which King was a member, charging branding cattle without first having a brand recorded; theft of a calf; and "pursuing occupation of Daguerrean, without taking out a license therefor."

At the next term, which convened May 3, 1875, Edward Dougherty, judge of another district, was on the bench by exchange with the new judge who had just been elected— a lawyer named Ware. W. R. Wallace was appointed district attorney *pro tem*, "the district attorney being absent."

The big news that came out of that 1875 term was an indictment against King Fisher and James Vivian, charged jointly with assault to murder one George Washington!

Vivian promptly posted a $500 bond, with Grey (Doc) White, C. N. Vivian, J. S. Vivian, and W. C. Bruton as sureties. Bill Bruton was released on $4,000 bond on a murder indictment.

Before the next term on September 6, 1875, Fisher made bond, his sureties having been J. H. Slaughter and W. T. Bruton. But when Fisher's case was called in September, he did not answer. The $500 bond was ordered forfeited, and capias for his arrest was ordered to be sent to Goliad and Bexar counties.

Bill Bruton was tried and acquitted in his murder case.

At that term King was indicted for illegally driving cattle, a misdemeanor, it being alleged that on June 25, 1875, he drove about two hundred head of cattle without the written authority of the owners, duly authenticated as required by law, "and the owner of said cattle being unknown to these grand jurors, and . . . without first having the same duly inspected . . ."

Evidently the King had decided to avoid going to trial. On January 3, 1876, when the next court convened, in referring to the last indictment the court ordered: "In this case it is ordered that it stand continued and that capias do issue to any county wherein defendant may be found."

The judge seemed determined to find him. A dozen warrants for his arrest were sent during the nine months that followed. He was sought in Kinney, Blanco, Maverick, Bexar, Goliad, Frio, Atascosa, Travis, and Karnes counties. Finally arrested in Maverick County, probably when he gave himself up, King promptly made bond, with LaFayette and James Vivian as sureties. A trial followed, and C. L. P. Johnston, the jury foreman, reported: "We the jury find the defendant not guilty as charged in the indictment."

Just why the King chose to avoid arrest and trial on his first two indictments is not clear. Making bond was an easy matter for him, and trying him at that time in Maverick County would have been an exercise in futility for the prosecutors. Perhaps he was busy elsewhere, moving cattle toward Kansas, or as a matter of strategy he may have thought it best to avoid arrest and trial for awhile and let the dust settle a bit. He employed former District Attorney Thomas Paschal to represent him, and also retained T. T. Teel—two of the best. The King always traveled first class.

The court that met at Eagle Pass appears to have done very little during the remainder of 1876.

Thomas Moore Paschal figured prominently in the affairs of court during the seventies in Maverick and Uvalde counties. He became judge in 1876, and continued to serve until 1892, when he was elected to the Fifty-third Congress. Born in Louisiana in 1845, he lived a checkered life, most of it in public service, and died in 1919.

Admitted to the bar in 1867, Paschal began to practice in San Antonio and he was later city attorney there; he then served as justice of the peace and U.S. commissioner for the West Texas district before moving to Castroville and becoming district attorney of the 24th Judicial District.

After being defeated for re-election, he moved to Brackettville where he practiced before going on the bench as district judge of the 24th District. He was defeated for Congress by Judge George H. Noonan, of San Antonio, a Republican, who was in turn defeated by James L. Slayden.

IX

The King Arrested

By THIS TIME the Texas Rangers were carrying the law to the chaparral, lending a new twist to local law enforcement. During the reconstruction period following the Civil War, lawlessness zoomed and enforcement was at an all-time low. Throughout Texas, scandal, inefficiency, and corruption characterized the feeble efforts to maintain law and order. An abortive attempt was made to establish a state police force in 1870. The reconstruction government installed political hacks in sheriff's offices, and pay-offs and favoritism were more the rule than the exception.

Indeed, reconstruction contributed a black page to Texas history. Texas was occupied by the U.S. forces on June 17, 1865, and a military government was imposed. The Lone Star State and Louisiana were put in the Fifth District, under command of General P. H. Sheridan, who followed a policy of crushing any alleged disloyalty in the area. Troops, including many Negroes, "carpetbaggers," and "scalawags," were put in control. At the whim of the military, many state and county officials were removed from office by Sheridan because he suspected that they were not in sympathy with the plans of the national Congress. Many weaklings and nondescripts were installed in their place.

Edmund J. Davis succeeded E. M. Pease as governor in 1869, with the support of the Grant administration. His election was made possible by disfranchising the Confederates and enfranchising the "freedmen," or former slaves. Davis was re-elected and kept the office until January 18, 1874.

He established a state police system in 1870, but in the main it was staffed by incompetents and hardly had a chance to function. In fact, because of its corruptness the State Police Law was repealed on April 22, 1873. Described as "an infernal engine of oppression," the State Police Law caused wide-spread rejoicing only when it was repealed [Farrow, *Troublesome Time in Texas*].

After two terms of blunders, Davis was defeated by Richard Coke in 1873. The state had grown weary of the Davis skullduggery. They were tired of the "buffalo soldiers" (Negro troops), and the people longed for honest police protection. The new governor was elected on a promise to restore law and order, and he proceeded to try to make good on that promise.

On May 2, 1874, Governor Coke commissioned John B. Jones, of Corsicana, a major in the Frontier Battalion. This was a smart move, marking a turning point, because a more competent man could not have been found for the job. Six companies of seventy-five men each were authorized, responsible only to Jones and the Governor.

Major Jones took command of the western frontier, and the Mexican border area was entrusted to Captain L. H. McNelly. The 14th Legislature appropriated $300,000 for frontier defense, and the best law-enforcement men obtainable were recruited. The Governor granted the Rangers authority to cross the Río Grande when necessary, a privilege which up to that time had not been granted to the U.S. Army.

From 1874 to 1880 the Rangers turned in their best performance. Unimpeded by county lines, they were free to pursue their prey wherever and whenever the occasion required. Mobs and feuds were active, adding to law-enforcement difficulties. The Taylor-Sutton feud in DeWitt County and the Horrell-Higgins feud in Lampasas were then in full swing. Stages were being held up, banks were robbed, and the Rangers had their hands full.

McNelly had his eye on King Fisher Territory, but there were other chores to see about before pushing up the Río Grande.

As the Rangers fingered their way into the hideaways of the ruffians who swarmed into southwest Texas, they were supplied with a booklet, called "the Book of Knaves," containing the names, aliases, and descriptions of some three thousand "wanted" men. It was said that not one in twenty of these were bona fide Texans. Mostly drifters, few of them were married. They lived by gambling, robbing, and stealing. The *Galveston News* of October 16, 1873, reported that in the town of Gonzales between 100 and 150 gamblers were counted in one room, and most of them were transients.

The gray, paper-backed booklet, which was also called the "Crime Book" and "Bible Two," was furnished to all Ranger camps. The names in the book were provided by sheriffs and by authorities from other states. They included men wanted for the most heinous of crimes, including murder, robbery, arson, burglary, rape, and common stealing. Rewards for some of them went as high as $10,000, according to Ranger N. A. Jennings.

These troopers were destined to rise to the heights of their glory during the "terrible seventies." Unique in the history of law enforcers, every Ranger was a volunteer and could quit at any time he desired. His duty was to face outlaws, including the embittered Indian, the Mexican *bandido*, and the native desperadoes, with the wanted men having the advantage of choosing the meeting place. It was said of the Ranger that "he could ride like a Mexican, trail like an Indian, shoot like a Tennesseean, and fight like the devil."

The Ranger's job included policing courts, safeguarding witnesses, escorting and protecting judges, and delivering his wanted men to the jail or cemetery, as the case might be. His jurisdiction was as wide as the boundaries of the state. And he sometimes crossed the Río Grande in "hot pursuit." With these responsibilities and this area to cover, the Rangers became an active, potent, and reliable force.

Unadorned with flashy uniforms such as characterized the Northwest Mounted Police, the Rangers favored ten-gallon hats and wore buckskin or corduroy trousers and good boots, usually cut straight across the tops. "He wore what he could get, and didn't have much of that," the late John W. Bracken, former Ranger, told Dora Raymond. Gold watches with chains attached were common possessions. He carried low-slung cartridge belts, with .45 Colts in scabbard, along with a bowie knife [Raymond, Dobie, Webb, and Durham].

In the seventies the Ranger preferred the 1873 Winchester, but since the weapon was not standard equipment, he paid for it himself if he carried it. The cost of the rifle plus forty dollars for ammunition could be deducted from his salary. The State furnished Sharps, or "Muley carbines," but the Winchester was a better gun. It carried more shells and was quicker to handle. Sharps, the old mainstay, were jocularly called "Beecher's Bibles," in memory of Reverend Henry Ward Beecher, who was not averse to a judicious amount of gunfire to advance a holy cause.

Most saddles were equipped with ox-bow stirrups. Each

man carried a Mexican blanket, a lariat, a small wallet for tobacco and ammunition and other extras. At night he used his saddle for a pillow and a layer of grass for a mattress; he put a gum coat over his equipment, placed a gun by his side, and usually slept with most of his clothes on.

The captains chose their own men and could discharge them at will. Careful to choose the brave and energetic, perfectly willing to risk their lives if and when required, the rangers were invariably men of strong personal character, strengthened by service on the force. The Rangers loved adventure, were top riders and sharp trailers, and were always ready to plunge into the thick of a fight.

Under the new setup, Captain McNelly recruited some of the toughest and most capable men in the state and set about to fight wholesale crime along the Mexican border. The Captain had been a Confederate, holding the rank of captain at the age of seventeen. After the war he came to Texas from Virginia and was put in charge of a Ranger company during the abortive reconstruction efforts to do something about lawlessness. In that assignment, though working under certain restraints, he overcame the handicaps to gain something of a reputation for efficiency.

Slight and consumptive, McNelly was nevertheless a man of extraordinary skill and a natural leader. His reputation made it easy for him to recruit the best men. Texans promptly forgave him for his association with the carpetbaggers, and McNelly lost no time in finding action. Completely devoid of fear, he treated his men as social equals, and every man in his outfit became devoted to him, almost to the point of fanaticism.

Kindly and suave in dealing with his men, the Captain allowed no swearing in his camp, and he maintained strict discipline in the discharge of commands.

71

McNelly's border activities were incredibly bold and fearless. Ignoring technicalities and warnings, he courted danger and always moved with speed and decision, regardless of the odds against him.

The Captain's intelligence service was most effective. He knew how to plant spies inside enemy lines, and he had an ingenious way of extracting vital information from prisoners.

Perhaps the most brazen peace-officer action ever undertaken on the Río Grande occurred in November, 1875, when McNelly, in hot pursuit of several hundred head of stolen cattle, stormed across the river with his company of steel-nerved lawmen. This violation of the border prompted General J. H. Potter, then in command of U.S. forces on the Río Grande, to wire Major Alexander, commander at the front where the crossing occurred:

> Advise Captain McNelly to return at once to this side of the river. Inform him that you are directed not to support him in any manner while he remains on Mexican territory. If McNelly is attacked by Mexican forces do not render him any assistance. Keep your forces in the position you now hold and wait further orders. Let me know if McNelly acts upon your advice and returns.

Las Cuevas was three miles from the river, opposite from Río Grande City, and was the headquarters of Juan Flores, leader of the cattle thieves in that vicinity. Years later Bill Callicott, one of the thirty Rangers in the group, recalled:

> We reached the ranch just at daylight. . . . Just before we got to the bars, Captain waited for us. . . . Old Casuse [Sandoval] pushed his hat to the back of his head, drew his pistol, rammed both spurs to his

old paint horse, gave a Comanche yell, and away the five men went shooting and yelling. . . . The rest of us closed in behind them, and if the angels of heaven had come down on that ranch the Mexicans would not have been more surprised. We were the first Rangers they had seen since the Mexican War.

It turned out that although this ranch harbored Cortina thieves it was not the headquarters the Rangers thought it was. The Las Cuevas stockade was a half mile away. Several Mexican bandits had been killed before the error was discovered. Undaunted by their exposure, the Rangers, most of them afoot, rushed to the main Las Cuevas where 250 Mexican soldiers were waiting, having heard the nearby shooting. A lively battle ensued, the action shrouded by heavy fog.

Confronted with this solid front of unexpected strength when the fog lifted, McNelly ordered a hasty retreat to the Río Grande. But instead of plunging into the raging waters to escape the oncoming troops, the resourceful McNelly cleverly concealed his men among the reeds and underbrush on the Mexican side and waited for the pursuers.

And come they did. It proved to be one of the cleverest and most audacious ambushes ever contrived on the border. Outnumbered nearly ten to one, the Texans were ready as the *Cortinistas* charged up to the riverbank, expecting to pick the Rangers off as they swam across. The first victim of the Captain's ruse was none other than General Juan Flores, the chieftain. After a flurry of Ranger bullets from concealed positions, the Mexicans retreated. During the battle, Sergeant Leakey, from the Texas side, had trained a Gatling gun on the bandits, and this may have turned the tide in McNelly's favor.

The Mexicans had charged three times, and Captain

Randlett, in command of the troops on the American side, believing that McNelly and his men were about to be massacred, and apparently ignoring orders, took thirty troopers across. Randlett had not yet delivered General Alexander's ultimatum to Captain McNelly and had that additional excuse for going over.

By then the Mexicans had withdrawn, but the move by Randlett must have impressed them with McNelly's apparent back-up support. The message was delivered, and without hesitation the Captain, using the brim of his hat for a desk, wrote out an answer which read:

> To General J. H. Potter, U.S.A., Fort Brown, Texas. I shall remain in Mexico with my Rangers until tomorrow morning, perhaps longer, and shall cross the Río Grande at my discretion. Give my compliments to the Secretary of War, and tell him the U.S. Troops may go to hell. L. H. McNelly, Commandg, Texas State Troops in Mexico [Durham, Farrow].

Although McNelly urged them to remain, the soldiers returned to the Texas side. The disorganized *Cortinistas*, having observed the troops, did not choose to resume the battle. Contact was made with the enemy, and McNelly agreed to retreat only after extracting a promise from the Mexicans to deliver the unrecovered stolen cattle to Río Grande City. The cattle were delivered under the armed direction of McNelly and his men and were then distributed to Captain King and other brand owners from whom they had been stolen.

After several bold and daring moves against the *Cortinistas*, including one at Las Cuevas and another at Palo Alto on the Texas side, during which thirteen bandits were killed, McNelly turned to the business of doing something about King Fisher.

Grass was knee high, and you could have heard the turtles sing when McNelly and his men headed up the border toward the Pendencia in May, 1876. Fresh from triumphs at Las Cuevas and Palo Alto, plus other less spectacular successes, the Captain must have regarded his new mission as something of a let-down. Ranger A. L. Parrott had already infiltrated the Fisher stronghold, posing as an itinerant photographer. After rejoining the company he told McNelly of how he had scouted the Territory, going from camp to camp, selling enlargements. He described the Fisher headquarters as "a right nice layout."

When McNelly informed his men of his plan to go into the Eagle Pass country for the first time, Sergeant Armstrong exclaimed: "Why that is King Fisher country. When we go in there somebody might get hurt!"

The Captain's enforcers at that time included the top lawmen of the southwest. Among them were Lieutenants L. B. Wright and T. J. Robinson; Sergeants R. P. Orrell, L. L. Wright, J. B. Armstrong, and George Hall; Corporals M. C. Williams and W. L. Rudd; Privates S. J. Adams, "Black" Allen, George Boyd, Bill Callicutt, T. N. Devine, George Durham, T. J. Evans, Matt Fleming, Griffen, B. Gorman, Andy Gourley, S. N. Hardy, N. A. Jennings, Horace Maben, A. C. Mackey, Thomas McGovern, John McNelly (the Captain's nephew), Thomas Melvin, Edward Mayers, Charles and W. W. McKinney, A. L. Parrott, T. M. Queensberry, J. S. Rock, H. J. Rector, W. O. Reichel, Horace Rowe, Jesus Sandoval, G. M. Scott, F. Siebert, L. S. Smith, G. W. Talley, W. T. Welch, and two others named Saldana and Jim Wofford.

Others whose names appear on the Captain's rolls at various times include privates named Nelson Gregory, "Cow" McKay, Jack Racy, D. R. Smith, N. R. Stegall,

T. Sullivan, Alfred Walker, James Williams, R. H. Wells, David Watson, and F. J. Williams.

McNelly was taking no chances. He was traveling first class, flanked by the most formidable assembly of lawmen in the country.

A stop was made at Carrizo Springs, near the famous Espantosa Lake. This was on the main wagon road which at that time extended from San Antonio west into the upper country and into northern Mexico. At Carrizo the Captain was briefed on the King Fisher movements by Levi English, the storekeeper. A youngster by the name of Drew Taylor was put on the Captain's payroll. Parrott had gained the young man's confidence, and he was made useful as a guide. After learning that the King was at home, McNelly took about twenty-five of his men and set out to make a surprise visit.

King Fisher was at that time twenty-two years of age and was at the peak of his power and influence. On April 6, 1876, the childhood romance between him and nineteen-year-old Sarah Vivian had culminated in marriage. Doc White, a devoted friend of both bride and groom, then justice of the peace in the Pendencia precinct, officiated, and undoubtedly gave the union his warmest blessing.

According to Durham, confirmed by Jennings who was also present, where the Pendencia road angled into the main road toward Eagle Pass, a few miles from the Fisher ranch, there was a sign which read: "This is King Fisher's Road—Take the other one."

The Rangers moved quietly toward the King's head-quarters. It was midday when they arrived. Two groups of them stormed into the front yard simultaneously, guns in hand. George Durham described the headquarters as nesting under cottonwood trees. A lean-to ran out from the north, and there was a saddle shed and picket fence out near the front. Several of Fisher's men were playing cards in the shed as the Rangers appeared.

The Captain had instructed his men not to fire unless active resistance was encountered. He had anticipated Fisher's wife would be there.

Frank Porter, one of the gang, was met by Parrott, who was promptly recognized as "that damn picture man."

"We're McNelly's Rangers," snapped Parrott.

Porter was in reality Burd Obenchain, from Kansas, who had fought with Quantrell's guerrillas and also had associated with the James brothers. He had tracked an enemy to Texas, caught up with him camped on the Espantosa Lake one night, murdered him, and then proceeded to eat the food his victim had cooked.

Parrott and Porter faced each other, each with rifle drawn, but neither saw fit to pull the trigger, although either could have done so with fatal results. The entire gang was arrested without either side firing a shot, and each of Fisher's men was disarmed. They included the King himself, Frank Porter, Warren Allen, Al Roberts, Bill and Wes Bruton, Bill Templeton, Bill Honecutt, and Bill Wainwright.

McNelly, according to Durham, who was present, ordered Fisher—who had emerged from inside the house—to lock his hands behind his head; and "right there, facing each other at not more than five paces, were by long odds the two best pistol fighters in Texas, before or since," said Durham.

King wore two of the fanciest pistols the Rangers had ever seen. Gold streaks showed on the grips, and the "hammers and barrels shined like glass," according to Durham.

There was no gun play. The King smiled as he handed his guns to the Captain, "The Captain smiled right back," reported Durham, "something I never saw him do to a man he wanted."

"We had you," said the Captain.

"Yes, you had me," Fisher replied, adding, "Pretty neat."

The biggest name on the Mexican border had surrendered peacefully. He was all smiles and confident. At this point the charming Sarah, a bride of two months, came out and demanded: "What are you doing to my husband?" McNelly calmly told her who he was and why he was there.

"What are you arresting him for? He's done nothing," she insisted.

King motioned her back inside, and added: "Shucks, Captain, I knew who you were the minute I saw you and you told me to give up. That's why I did. I'm a law-abiding man."

The Pendencia ranchman then wanted to know what he had done, what he was charged with.

Later both Durham and Jennings wrote books about their experiences on the border with McNelly [Jennings, Durham]. Jennings was clerk for the company, and helped prepare the official reports that were sent to the Adjutant General Steele. Being a writer, Jennings had a flare for the spectacular, and his reports were embellished at times to make them more readable. But the basic facts as given by the two Rangers appear to be consistent. Jennings was an experienced writer and was very observant of details. Hence, his description of the King must be assumed to be reasonably accurate:

Fisher was . . . the most perfect specimen of a frontier dandy and desperado I ever met. He was tall,
beautifully proportioned, and exceedingly handsome.
He wore the finest clothing procurable, but all of the
picturesque, border, dime-novel kind. His broad-

brimmed white Mexican *sombrero* was profusely ornamented with gold and silver lace and had a golden
snake for a band. His fine buckskin Mexican short
jacket was heavily embroidered with gold. His shirt
was of the finest and thinnest linen and open at the
throat, with a silk handkerchief knotted loosely about
the wide collar. A brilliant crimson sash was wound
about his waist, and his legs were hidden by a won-
derful pair of *chaparejos*, or chaps as cowboys called
them—leather breeches, to protect the legs while riding through the brush.

The surprise visit evidently caught the King preparing to
attend a fandango, or perhaps he was trying on a new
outfit.

Jennings went on to explain that the *chaparejos* were
made of the skin of a royal Bengal tiger and ornamented
down the seams with gold and buckskin fringe. The tiger
skin, according to the writing Ranger, had been procured
at a circus. While this detail may or may not be a correct
recitation of the facts, it would seem only natural that
Jennings, every bit a journalist, would in typical reporter-
style have been inquisitive about where that tiger came
from since such mammals did not range in that country.
According to Jennings some of Fisher's crowd captured the
circus and killed and skinned the tiger because the King
wanted to make use of the skin.

Jennings said a cartridge-filled belt and two ivory-
handled silver-plated six-shooters adorned the King, and
his description is similar to that of Durham. His spurs, reported Jennings, were of silver and ornamented with little
silver bells.

Durham, in his report, noted that at that time King Fisher
had spread far and wide—"over most of the Nueces country

and clear to San Antonio." King was not, as Durham saw it, a rowdy barroom killer. "In fact," the Ranger continued, "he was noted as a teetotaler. He killed clean and with either hand; he was one of the genuine two-pistol fighters."

The prisoners were handcuffed, then lashed to their saddles as they were put astride their mounts for the long trip to Eagle Pass. Their feet were tied to the stirrups, their hands to the pommels of their saddles, and the escorting Rangers led the horses. As they were about to depart, the Captain made it a point to inform Fisher's wife that the prisoners were to be taken to Eagle Pass, and that if any rescue was attempted along the way all the captives would be killed. This was known as *la ley de fuga*, the shooting of escaping or resisting prisoners. Sarah, "whose black eyes flashed angrylike," said to the Ranger Captain:

"That's your law. We've heard you make your own law, but let me tell you . . . if you kill my husband . . ."

"No rescue will be attempted," Sarah assured. "My husband has done nothing and you can't keep him in jail."

The border chieftain, casual and fully composed, calmly told his wife to do as directed, to get word to any of his friends of what McNelly had said.

Lieutenant Wright and six Rangers were detailed to take the prisoners to the county seat. McNelly, then suffering from advanced tuberculosis, was not equal to the trip by horseback. He ordered his hack, then called an "ambulance," which took him, accompanied by his wife, to Eagle Pass, where he arrived at noon the following day. The prisoners were put in jail, but King's attorney was waiting for him.

The Captain informed Deputy Sheriff Vale that he was turning the nine men over to him. A discussion followed, during which the lawyer made much of the fact that there was no new charge against Fisher, except suspicion, and that if they were to be held some specific charges, backed by witnesses, would have to be produced.

"The Captain was whipped," wrote Durham later.

As the attorney lectured them on conformity with the written code, not the "jungle law," as he chose to call it, Durham slapped him severely, and the Captain ordered the offending Ranger outside.

McNelly then informed Vale that Kansas had felony warrants for two of the prisoners—Frank Porter and Wes Bruton, and that Missouri wanted three of the others. But the Captain had no warrants—only their names and descriptions in the Crime Book, then carried by all Rangers. This, McNelly insisted, was tantamount to a blanket warrant.

The lawyer challenged the validity of the "warrants," and the deputy wanted assurance that the other states would come for the prisoners and pay the expenses of holding them. McNelly, obviously miffed by the road block and the technicalities that had been thrown at him, in disgust turned to Wright and ordered: "Give these men back their guns and release them!"

At that point the Captain gave Fisher some advice. It was quite evident the famous Ranger was impressed by the hotspur's personality and felt impelled to appeal to the better side of his nature. A few years later King had occasion to refer to that lecture and the impression it must have made on him.

"You've won," conceded McNelly, according to Durham.

You're a young man, King. You've won every bout with the law up to now. You just might be lucky and win some more, but finally you'll lose one and that one will be for keeps. At least it will be if you lose to the

Rangers. We don't fight draw or dogfalls. When we lose, we lose. When we win, we win. And when we win once, that's enough. The law might lose now and then. We just did. But the law always wins the last round. We'll win. We represent the law.

The King, flushed with victory, insisted that he was a law-abiding citizen.

"Make sure you stay law-abiding, King. You've got a nice wife. You could make a good citizen. You'd also make a nice corpse. All outlaws look good dead."

McNelly probably sensing that he was making some headway with his gratuitous lecture, continued:

". . . I only aimed to tell you to get out of this outlaw business. The next time the Rangers come after you we just might leave you where we overhaul you—and you could make a better life for yourself. But it's up to you."

Thus ended the first arrest by Rangers of King Fisher, king of the border country. An abortive one, it nevertheless served to set in motion a series of arrests and court actions that made border history during the ensuing three years. Whether the King sensed it or not, the law had at last come to the chaparral. There was a change in the air.

There remained the matter of reporting to the adjutant general. Dated June 4, 1876, a telegram from Eagle Pass stated:

HAVE ARRESTED KING FISHER AND NINE OF HIS GANG AND TURNED THEM OVER TO SHERIFF. WILL CAMP AT FORT EWELL AND SCOUT COUNTRY BETWEEN HERE AND OAKVILLE UNTIL OTHERWISE INSTRUCTED. COUNTRY IN MOST DEPLORABLE CONDITION. ALL CIVIL OFFICERS HELPLESS.

This report was supplemented by another one in more

detail, one that painted a dire picture of King Fisher Territory:

> You can scarcely realize the true conditions of the section. The country is under a perfect reign of terror. . . . The country is rich in stock, but very sparsely settled, and the opportunities and inducements to steal are very great. . . .
>
> About one-half of the white citizens of Eagle Pass are friends of King Fisher's gang. The remainder of the citizens are too much afraid of the desperadoes to give any assistance in even keeping them secure after they have been placed in jail, and they would never think of helping to arrest any of them. . . .
>
> No witnesses can be found who will dare testify against the desperadoes and I am told by the Circuit Judge that he is convinced no jury in three counties— Dimmit, Maverick, and Live Oak—can be found to convict them. . . .

McNelly was a sick man. Jim Wofford was driving his hack, and he told others the boss was coughing up blood. The Rangers rode back to the temporary camp they had established at Carrizo Springs before the Pendencia raid. The Captain followed.

The arrest and release had served to add to King's laurels. He became recognized as more of a hero than ever, at least among his loyal partisans.

Things were buzzing around Carrizo when the lawmen arrived there. A *baile* was scheduled, a big social event in those parts, and people came in from the country for the *fiesta*.

"King Fisher came down from the Pendencia," reported Durham. "Every inch a king, something to blink your eyes at. He rode a deep-chested dapply gray gelding that would

83

heft around twelve hundred pounds, a lively prancing piece of horseflesh that had plenty of Kentucky breeding in him. His only blemish was a burned brand, that had ended up as a 7D."

The Ranger went on to describe the saddle, carved out of flank leather, and about "ten pounds of beat silver." King, in all his regal splendor, was capped with a brown beaver—the kind built for a cattle king or bandit king. And the Ranger then proceeded to describe the other gear, including the Bengal *chaparejos*, taken from the circus.

When Captain and Mrs. McNelly arrived at camp, Mc-Nelly did not leave his vehicle. The next morning he turned his command over to Lieutenant Robinson and ordered him to move the group to Oakville. The Captain proceeded to San Antonio. After eight days at Carrizo, the company, then composed of twenty-five men, pulled out, leaving the redoubtable King in control.

Durham emphasized that King Fisher was not the type to resist the law when faced with men in authority. "He'd give up to a Mexican burro if it had a Ranger badge," he said. "All the good I could see come of it was to give some Rangers the chance to tell their young'uns they'd arrested King Fisher."

The Carrizo settlement at that time was described by the Ranger as being somewhat different from others in that there were no saloons. There was no law against anyone selling liquor, but still it was not being done in the Pendencia's neighboring town of Carrizo Springs. Why? "That," the Ranger added, "was King Fisher's law—no saloons, or drinking. And we heard he was lots harder on a bootlegger than he was on a stagecoach robber or a stock rustler."

Durham, one of the most rugged and dedicated on the

force, was admittedly impressed with what he had seen of the King.

I had heard of him and now I was face to face with him, my eyes popped out. He was the most command-ing picture I had ever seen. He stood six foot, and weighed, I judge, 180 pounds. He had black, wavy hair; and while he was just turning twenty-one years of age, he was growing one of them mustaches that he trained down his cheek.

He wore a *tres piedras sombrero*, with a solid gold, coiled rattler, for a band; and gold tassles. His shirt was of that heavy Mexico City silk, opened at the throat; and a silk, red bandana was knotted around his neck.

X
Lee Hall Takes Over

THUS, BY 1876 there was indeed a change in the air. The
Texas Rangers had made their first intrusion into King
Fisher Territory—and it was not to be the last. They had
moved into the Nueces Strip and had challenged the King
in his own domain. The year witnessed significant developments on both sides of the Río Grande. On the other side
Porfirio Díaz gained power, and Juan Cortina was on the
defensive, soon to become a prisoner of the Mexican government.

After leaving Carrizo Springs, the Rangers proceeded to
Oakville, and McNelly went on to San Antonio for medical attention. At Oakville on August 10, 1876, Lieutenant
Hall joined the company and was placed second to McNelly
in command. The men were a little fretful about the intrusion, most of them thinking that if the Captain was going
to be replaced the honor should have gone to either Robinson or Armstrong, both veterans. Sergeant Armstrong, a
mustached Kentuckian, was known as "McNelly's bulldog,"
and both of these men were very popular.

Oakville was at that time a hot spot. One hundred men,
including forty local citizens, had been violently killed there
during the preceding decade. Life was rather cheap around
Oakville.

Before Hall's arrival, another trip toward Espantosa

Lake was shaping up, under Armstrong, by McNelly's orders. And the thrust was destined to be very rewarding.

This scouting expedition consisted of twenty-five men. Reports had been persistent of the movement of stolen horses and cattle through the Espantosa country, in the heart of King Fisher's country. A one-hundred-mile ride, including night travel, added surprise to the maneuver, a typical Ranger technique.

By the second night the Rangers were back at Carrizo, arresting everyone they chanced to meet. One Noley Key was induced to disclose details of a bunch of East Texas horses being held at the lake for later delivery on Devil's River. The King, Key confided, had left two days earlier with a herd of 150 steers, moving toward West Texas. Six Rangers were sent out to scout the area where the horses were supposed to be; the group was composed of Rangers Devine, Evans, Boyd, Parrott, Jennings, and Durham. The gang of horse wranglers were surprised in camp at night. An open battle ensued, with some hand-to-hand combat, and seven bandits were killed.

Doc White, justice of the peace, was notified about the bodies, and the Rangers sent twenty-two prisoners to Eagle Pass, then continued collecting others.

George Durham, who wrote about this famous skirmish, was cautious to report that the King may or may not have been connected with the gang of outlaws who were surprised and killed that night. "Maybe King Fisher was head and brains of this stock-rustling bunch," he said. "I don't know. All I know is that we never did make a case on him. I want to set the record straight on that."

The Espantosa Lake was a likely place for a bloody encounter such as the Rangers were involved in. That night McNelly's men added to the legend that surrounds that body of water.

Frank Dobie has written that Espantosa means "frightful" and "phantasmal," and others refer to it as a "ghost" lake. According to Dobie the mystery of the spot:

> . . . began away back in early times, as the story goes, [when] some families from Mexico on their way to San Antonio camped here for several days in order to recruit their horses. One evening while a woman was washing clothes at the water's edge, no doubt squatted and rubbing them on a rock, men in camp heard a wild and horrifying cry. They rushed down, but all they saw was a streak of blood and the slash of a great scaled tail. *"Dios, es un largarto!"* (God, it is an alligator), one exclaimed. The next morning they erected a cross at the spot where the woman had disappeared. Some of them claimed to hear the cries again the next dusk. They left the place, and the lake with its name, Espantosa.

Speaking of the lake, George Durham later explained that it was actually an old channel or cut-off of the Nueces, almost half a mile wide and ten miles long at that time, and was named Espantosa because of its many alligators. The gators devoured the bodies of men or animals dumped into the lake, and many travelers were said to have vanished in this area.

The Ranger explained further that the Lake of Ghosts received its name because of reports that robbers had taken all the valuables from their victims and then dropped the victims in the lake, and that some of the victims' ghosts came back every moonlit night and walked around on the waters.

Indeed for generations tragedy and mystery had haunted the lake and its environs. In 1836 remnants of Dr. Charles Beales's ill-fated Dolores colonizing effort below Brackettville, en route to San Patricio, were encamped at Lake Espantosa. Numbering fourteen adults and three children, the group concealed themselves in the brush to avoid being seen by passing Mexican troops, presumably Santa Anna's. By April 2 the convoy had disappeared, and the transients fished at the lake. But the lake was Espantosa, and tragedy stalked the party's innocent movements.

After supper on that day, the women and children went a little way from the men and bathed. As they bathed Indians surprised the men and killed all of them, and the survivors spent the night hiding in the chaparral. Returning the next morning, they found the camp destroyed, with equipment and clothing torn to pieces or thrown into the deep waters. With no food and their clothes in tatters, they moved eastward, and three days later were intercepted by a small band of friendly Indians, who shortly released them to some passing Anglos. The children and one of the women had died.

This was but one incident associated with Espantosa and was preceded by many other tragedies that made the Spaniards call the lake "fearful" and "frightful." *El Camino Real*, for two centuries serving as the main passageway from Mexico to Texas, passed near the lake, accounting for the many adventurers who soon learned to approach that body of water with much trepidation.

As late as the 1880's Mexicans living in Carrizo Springs steadfastly refused to camp on or near the lake at night. They insisted it was haunted.

Santa Anna's army, marching toward the Alamo from Saltillo, Monclova, and the Presidio del Río Grande, came to Espantosa in mid-February of 1836. Ill-equipped, untrained, and plagued with dysentery, the Mexican soldiers sought stock water at the lake for the 1,800 pack mules—an outfit that looked more like a freight convoy than an army of fighting men. Halting their two-wheeled carts, four-wheeled wagons, and other vehicles and animals, the large party rested at Espantosa, thus giving rise to more legends of cannon, wagons, and even Spanish gold being dumped into the cool waters or buried on the banks of the lake.

Reporting on the Espantosa fight, Sergeant Armstrong in October, 1876, advised the adjutant general that after the fight it was learned from one of the wounded that there was a "bad" Mexican at Whaley's ranch, eight miles away.

Three Rangers were sent to the ranch, but "He refused to surrender," according to the sergeant, "and fought desperately until our men were obliged to kill him in self-defense."

The report went on to say that "there are numerous bad characters in the country, but they keep hidden in the brush so that it is difficult to find them." He added that King Fisher had left about one week earlier with a large drove of cattle, and that Frank Porter was supposed to be with him. This report evidently was based upon information given by Noley Key.

Armstrong also said that the accosted bandits had about fifty head of stolen stock near the scene of the Espantosa battle. After collecting weapons from the dead, the Rangers returned to their horses, learning from the Ranger left behind guarding a prisoner that while the shooting was taking place nearby the horses had become excited and the prisoner had attempted to escape. After being three times ordered to halt "he kept running and was fired upon and killed."

Years later these incidents were related by Durham to Clyde Wantland, who recorded them for history. No man was better able to speak about Leander H. McNelly than was Durham. His appraisal of the incomparable Captain is noteworthy:

Lee Hall was a good man, but he wasn't a Captain McNelly. I served under Hall, and I've worked for a good many other Ranger captains through the years. Captain McNelly wasn't the only topnotch man who ever commanded a company of Texas Rangers, but there was never another one like him—and never another one I thought as much of. I've thanked his memory a thousand times because he taught me tricks in gun fighting and law enforcement that have stood me in good stead for more than half a century as a peace officer. And he taught me a respect for the law that kept me on the right side.

Evincing a respect, if not admiration, for King Fisher, Durham was one of the few authorities who insisted that the Pendencia leader was not half as bad as often depicted:

I am not trying to excuse King Fisher for anything he done, and I reckon he done plenty. But I have had arguments all my life over him and I have made some of the McNelly men fighting mad because I stuck up for King. I throwed down on him and arrested him once, yes; and so did some of the other Rangers. But, damn if I don't still say that King was a better man than some that arrested him. He was all man; and that is more than I can say for at least one that bragged all his life about arresting him.

In the meantime, McNelly's condition worsened. Dr. Cupples, of San Antonio, who was treating him, had found his condition unimproved since the preceding October; he was suffering from "complete disability." Long hours in all sorts of weather had taken a heavy toll.

When the company was reorganized, McNelly's name was left off the roster. This omission created quite a stir, but Adjutant General Steele pointed to the Captain's failing health and proceeded to lay the facts before the public. To justify his action, Steele published McNelly's medical bill, showing it was one-third of the cost of maintaining the entire company. Moreover, Steele added, Lee Hall then in command was "in the full vigor of early manhood and health," and he reminded the public that the new company included the best men of McNelly's force—and would cost only half as much.

The retiring Captain, than whom no greater officer ever served on the Texas Ranger force, died on September 4, 1877, at the age of thirty-three. He was buried in Washington County where a tall shaft was erected over the grave by a friend and admirer, Captain Richard King.

McNelly's last recorded service was in October, 1876, when he and five of his men traveled to Clinton to escort five of the Sutton gang who had been indicted for murdering Dr. Philip Brazell and his son in one of the most heinous and inexcusable crimes ever committed.

The year 1877 was a good year for Lee Hall—and a bad year for those who got in his way. After taking command, Hall lost no time planning a massive sweep of the border country, to culminate in the heart of King Fisher Territory—Eagle Pass. He had quietly contacted various citizens, laid the groundwork for their grand jury service, and timed his drive to reach Maverick County on the eve of the spring term of the court, scheduled to meet on May 15, 1877.

In a dispatch from Eagle Pass, dated February 13, 1877, Sergeant John B. Armstrong had reported to Steele that two days earlier Charles Bruton had been stopped at Fort Clark and thirty-nine uninspected cattle cut out of a herd he was driving. The other cattle were released.

In the same report he said King Fisher was back on the Pendencia and "is gathering a crowd around him again." The report said Fisher and his men had many horses hobbled around their camps and again complained about the difficulty of getting witnesses to testify against the King "or any of his clan."

But on May 18, Hall sent Steele an encouraging report of the Eagle Pass situation.

> . . . We were warmly received by the people in this county, who looked upon our arrival as truly a godsend just at this time, as in no section of the state have the good people and the law been worse trampled by desperadoes and thieves than in this County and Dimmit which is attached. . . . Three months since I scoured the list of Grand Jurors for the County and have endeavored to impress each of them previous to assembling of the Court that they would be amply protected against the numerous outlaws and desperadoes who for a long while have had full sway in this community.

Hall reported that as a result of his efforts the alerted citizens were doing their full duty; that indictments had been returned against King Fisher and others who "have gone scot free heretofore, though several Grand Juries have been held here since they have been guilty of the most heinous crimes known to the law, committed even in the presence of officers of the law."

Hall complimented Judge Thomas Paschal and John Sullivan, then district attorney, and gave them credit for full co-operation.

He reported that in a sweep up the border he and his men had made thirty-three arrests but had released ten or twelve "as they had fled from the direction of Kimble County where Major Jones has lately been operating." He added that some of these were difficult to identify and hold.

"We have taken bond and have under arrest at this time twenty-one with a certainty of a number more of arrests before we leave this place. . . ."

Referring to King Fisher, the Captain in his May 18 report noted: "I think there will be a change of venue in King Fisher's cases, of whose arrest I telegraphed you. (The arrest occurred May 16, 1877.) My men are now engaged in guarding the jail, bringing in witnesses and protecting them in appearing before the Grand Jury."

XI

More Court Troubles

THE MAVERICK COUNTY GRAND JURY, of which Charles H. Vivian was foreman, was empaneled in May, 1877. It indicted King for murder in the first degree and filed another true bill against W. C. Bruton on the charge of assault to murder. Fisher's case (No. 172) was promptly set down for trial, and a special venire was ordered. But on May 18, a significant order was entered by Judge Paschal. Because "no jury can probably be had in the County of Maverick for the trial . . . and . . . there are . . . influences existing in Maverick County in favor of said defendant," the Judge changed the venue to Uvalde County.

The indictment charged King with the murder of one William Dunovan by shooting him three times with a pistol, in the unorganized county of Zavala, the crime alleged to have occurred on December 25, 1876.

T. T. Teel, King's attorney, later, after King was killed, insisted the charge was unfounded.

On the same date three additional indictments were filed against Fisher—charging him with three instances of horse stealing. His bondsmen were George Whaley, B. C. Flowers, C. L. Fielder, José Oliva, Francisco Zertouche, LaFayette Vivian, and Charles H. Vivian—all among the wealthier and more prominent citizens of the county.

The May term of court had been a sort of personal triumph for Lee Hall. He had scoured the county in advance and button-holed prospective jurors, urging indictments against King Fisher. A personable man, Hall gained the confidence of the local people. His Ranger contingent moved about with an air of confidence, reassuring the timid and bolstering the willing. He induced the county judge and commissioners to expose themselves to backlash by sending an appeal to Governor Hubbard in Austin.

In a letter to the Governor on May 15, the Judge and four commissioners told him that after District Court adjourned there would probably be some dangerous prisoners left in the local jail which would require guards, which the county could ill afford to pay. They called for a detachment of Rangers to be kept in Eagle Pass.

> We also wish to express the confidence we feel in Lieut. Hall and his company and to testify the obligation that we feel under to them for the assistance that they have given us, and are still affording. Their presence having inspired our officers and the people generally with confidence, and we feel that the many indictments found by the Grand Jury now in session, and the three arrests made, are largely due to their presence and valuable assistance.

At the next court term in July, Judge Paschal in ordering a prisoner transferred to Uvalde noted that "the jail of Maverick County is insecure."

Lee Hall was relentless. He was determined to put King Fisher out of business. Indictments, with or without convictions, which authorized arrests and harassment, were components in his strategy to keep the alleged violators on the defensive.

Before the dust could settle, following the May term, Hall had organized another roundup. On July 30, 1877, "with his pockets bulging with warrants," Hall and his Rangers again rode out from Castroville. Destination: Eagle Pass and King Fisher Territory.

En route they stopped over at Frio City, where Captain Neal Coldwell and his Ranger detachment were encamped. They were joined at that point by still another detachment of eighteen under Sergeant George Arrington. With this entourage, split into groups, they swooped down again upon Eagle Pass.

A number of suspects were lodged in the local jail. News of the new sweep even spread across the border, causing "alarms and excursions," and quite an exodus was reported from the border towns. A detachment marched down the river. On August 6, Hall and his men arrested forty of Valdes' men and found among them four murderers and three horse thieves for whom they had warrants. There is, however, no evidence the Valdes gang bore any relationship to the King Fisher establishment.

The groundwork had been laid by Hall, and his influence over the local populace was proved anew when the court met in November. The King was indicted for murder in five cases—jointly with others in one of the charges. Hall's strategy was paying off. He wanted indictments, and he got them.

Most of the offenses charged against Fisher were alleged to have occurred as much as two years earlier. He was accused of killing a Mexican named Estanislado and another named Pancho—both employed by Alexander Zimmerman, a ranchman in Dimmit County. The time: November 10, 1875—two years before the indictments were returned. King was also charged with killing one Severin Flores.

In the latter case Fisher was taken into custody on November 19, 1877, and was lodged in the county jail of

Bexar County. Here was a new tactic—getting the prisoner beyond the sphere of his influence and control. There, in the "Bat Cave," as the old San Antonio jail was called, the King languished until April 11, 1878, just under five months. In April he was finally released to the sheriff of Medina County for a habeas corpus hearing before Judge Paschal at Castroville.

The Bat Cave was very much a part of the early history of old San Antonio. Built in 1850, it served as jail, city hall, and courthouse for thirty years, until the new city hall was built in the center of Military Plaza. Its name was derived from the fact that bats inhabited the second floor where district court was held, and had to be driven out when the judge appeared. In the rear of the building was the jail, surrounded by a high wall, the top of which was crowned with imbedded glass from broken bottles to prevent escape.

The building was also used by civic and religious bodies and was the initial gathering place for Baptists in the area. The Vigilantes of the Civil War held meetings there, and the Belknap Rifles, a famous San Antonio rifle team, held their organizational meeting in the old Bat Cave.

On one notable occasion when a man being tried for a crime, a Bob Augustine, was found not guilty, he was dragged out the window by irate citizens who did not agree with the verdict and hanged to a chinaberry tree on the Plaza.

After the new city hall was built, the Bat Cave was used as a recorder's court (Police Judge) and jail, and soon fell into bad repair. It held, in its time, many prisoners, and was usually shown to visiting tourists. Once, shortly before the building was razed, a party of eastern tourists drove up in a hack and asked the policeman at the door: "What old mission is this?" King Fisher's having slept there added to its appeal as a tourist attraction.

The reason why a habeas corpus hearing was not had at an earlier date is not clear. King was represented by the most capable lawyers to be found, and the charges against him were clearly bondable. It is quite likely that the Judge was in no hurry to entertain the motion, and the lawyers did not see fit to press the application which had been filed on December 21, 1877.

When the hearing was finally held, in the Judge's chambers, an impressive group of witnesses was sought. Some were found, others were not. Bond was promptly granted.

"It is the opinion of the Court that applicant is entitled to bail and his bail is hereby fixed at $25,000."

Bail bond was signed by such prominent ranchmen as George Whaley, B. C. Flowers, C. L. Fielder, José Angel Oliva, Francisco Zertouche, and LaFayette and Charles Vivian. Bonds in other cases were also set, at $2,500 each, and were promptly made, and the King returned to the Pendencia.

As it turned out, no additional indictments were ever returned against Fisher following the November, 1877, term of court. The climax in Hall's battle to crack King's stranglehold on King Fisher Territory was reached at that time.

All told, there were some fifteen indictments then pending in Maverick County against the Pendencia chieftain, including those sent to Uvalde on changes of venue.

When the spring term of court opened in Eagle Pass on May 13, 1878, suspense was in the air. Judge Paschal was on hand, as was District Attorney Sullivan. A new county clerk, Charles Schmidt, had taken office in January. A. M. Oliphant, the county attorney, also made an appearance.

In addition, there was an array of attorneys, numbering eight. Several of these, including T. T. Teel, were there to represent Fisher.

On the opening day the grand jurors reported, including LaFayette and James Vivian, but the latter was excused. Four of the men who had been summoned for grand jury service failed to answer. Only five answered. And of the petit jurors on call, eighteen, including John Vivian, could not be found by the sheriff.

The next day the Judge became irked by the shortage of chairs in the crowded courtroom and made his feelings known with this stern order:

> It being manifest to the Court that there is a deficiency of seats in the Courthouse to properly accommodate the bar, officers of the Court, citizens and witnesses during the trial of causes, it is ordered that this deficiency be notified to the Honorable County Commissioners Court now in session and that they be requested forthwith to furnish the District Court room with one dozen substantial chairs and that this order be forthwith certified by the clerk to said Commissioners Court and that the Sheriff present the chairs so furnished at the earliest possible moment.

The minutes are silent on the result of the Judge's order for more chairs and also on just what he could have done to the commissioners had they not responded.

The court was thrown into an uproar the first day when the district attorney arose to disclose that the "indictments and all other papers" in thirty-one pending cases were missing! The court took sworn statements from former clerk Albert Turpe concerning the missing records, and Charles B. H. Schmidt, the present clerk, confirmed the attorney's report and ordered that the district attorney "do have permission to substitute for the original copies. . . ."

The missing papers included seven cases against King Fisher, five of them for murder.

On May 20 the King made bond in six cases—one for $5,000; three for $2,500 each; and two for $1,200. The same seven men signed each bond.

A week earlier, on May 14, the murder case against King, charging him with killing Estanislado, was called for trial, and the court entered the following on his docket:

"In this case, it appearing to the Court that no attorney can be found in this County to prosecute this cause, in behalf of the State, and therefore no trial can be had and it appearing to the Court that attorneys for defendant and the State (by A. M. Oliphant who represents the State only for the purpose of changing venue), having agreed to the change of venue to Uvalde County," it was so ordered.

In the meantime, the King was indicted in Webb County. The grand jury at Laredo had charged him with six instances of horse stealing. At the April term, 1877, the grand jury there alleged he took horses belonging to Nicolas Sanchez, and in five of the alleged offenses the date of taking was the same—February 17, 1877. A total of seventy-eight horses was involved.

Court records indicate the horses were found in or near Fisher's camp on the Chicon Creek, near Laredo. The horses had been running on the open range, and a witness said the trail was followed "forty odd leagues from the range to the horses in the vicinity of King Fisher's camp where they were found." Others were also charged with taking some of the animals. The evidence of guilt was obviously circumstantial and inconclusive. Incidentally, one

101

Margarito Sanchez was foreman of the grand jury which returned the indictments.

Later the King was tried before juries at Laredo on three of the cases, and in each he was found not guilty. The other three were dismissed. He was represented in Laredo by T. T. Teel.

XII

Trials—and Reform

"They say best men are moulded out of faults, and, for the most, become much more the better for being a little bad!"—Shakespeare, *Measure for Measure*.

THE YEAR OF DECISION came in 1879. The King had reached the crescendo of his dominance. Lawyer fees were high, and the border leader was maturing in both age and experience with the law. Ranger overtures to induce him to leave his domain, as terms of a settlement, were spurned. Lee Hall's determination, evidenced by his tampering with grand jurors—a practice countenanced then but which would be questioned today—had paid off with a multiplicity of indictments. It appeared that the resourceful Ranger figured on arresting and indicting the King out of business—when it seemed all else failed.

Plain-spoken George Durham, reminiscing in the Harlingen *Valley Morning Star* about Hall and his early command of the company, wrote: "Lee Hall took command; and Lee thought to make a reputation he had to do something to King Fisher. He kept sending over the details to arrest King.

"Well, damn it, he didn't have any case on King. He stood trial on that Daugherty killing and came clear. They proved that the two men was sworn enemies; that they met on the prairie and it was a swap-out; and King won."

103

The former Ranger then recalled a time when Hall sent him and Ranger Parrott back to Eagle Pass. They found Fisher in Wes Bruton's saloon.

"Reckon you boys want me," said King.

"Yes," replied Parrott, "we got papers for you."

Durham said King unbuckled his belt, handed over his guns, and bought a drink, then told the Rangers if they wanted to take in some of the fandangos or Mexican dances that night he would be glad to take them along and show them the night life of the town. They went and reported a good time. "The next morning we locked King up in jail and left."

Before leaving, the Rangers picked up a youngster in Bruton's saloon.

"He was from the East, like our man Jennings, and had him some new pistols," recalled Durham, "and hairy pants and such stuff and had come down to help the Rangers capture King Fisher. He was drinking a little mescal and getting pretty loud, and I knowed if we left him in Eagle Pass he would get killed, so I arrested him and we herded him back to Cuero; and he promised he would go back home to his folks and forget them wild dreams he had of blasting down King Fisher and helping the Rangers."

The Ranger recalled that when nothing came of the thrust against Fisher, Lee Hall once sent Ranger Allen to do a better job. Allen arrested King, roped him to a mule, and started to Laredo with him.

"King didn't like this so much," the Ranger said, "so down the river a piece, he stompeded the pack animals; and when Allen and his two men run for them, King dived his mule into the river and crossed to Mexico."

Durham said the escape resulted in some embarrassing

publicity, "and I was damn glad. Because King was a better man than Allen."

During the year of decision, 1879, Fisher was content to let the dust settle. He busied himself with personal affairs, and there were no court actions against him. His name and his reputation were, however, still in the forefront. An unfounded rumor was circulated that year to the effect that Fisher had accidentally shot himself. This prompted the *Austin Statesman* to treat the incident in a derisive vein:

> King Fisher, the desperado of former years is now a quiet, placable, industrious rancher. He began to feel the devil getting the better of him a few days ago and rather than have any trouble or shoot anybody else, he shot himself through the thigh and is now lying up to cool off. He may be a priest yet. There is nothing like self punishment and "mortification of the spirit," if you don't have to submit to amputation.

The year of 1879 was also a year of decision for Lee Hall's Ranger force. The company had been plagued by shortage of funds to finance its operations. Diminished funds had forced the company down to fifteen privates and two sergeants the preceding October. And on January 2, the company was mustered out. In East Texas, where the Rangers were not so popular, there was rejoicing. But public pressure was brought to bear on Governor O. M. Roberts.

Bills from merchants in the Southwest who had supplied Hall's outfit totaled $46,000. When the legislature finally appropriated funds for the Rangers, the Governor vetoed the bill. The Ranger force had become deeply involved in politics.

Those great alligators, the State legislators,
Are puffing and blowing two-thirds of the time,

But windy orations about rangers and rations
Never put in our pockets one-tenth of a dime.

They do not regard us, they will not reward us,
Though hungry and haggard with holes in our coats;
But the election is coming and they will be drumming
And praising our valor to purchase our votes.

Then in July, at a special session of the legislature, more money was finally voted, and this time it received the Governor's approval. The appropriations bill called for the mustering in of a Special Force for the Suppression of Crime and Lawlessness, with Lee Hall in command, under Major John B. Jones.

The reorganization of the company was completed in July, and twenty-seven men, most of them veterans, were sworn in.

Captain Lee Hall's career as a Ranger was now drawing near its close. The following year, 1880, at the age of twenty-nine, he resigned to marry Miss Bessie Weidman, a San Antonio beauty.

Born October 9, 1849, Hall had received an education and taught school in his native North Carolina before proceeding to Denison, Texas, then called "the Gateway to Texas." As a young deputy sheriff in that habitué of bad men, the newcomer, although then only twenty-three years of age, achieved a reputation for rash bravery and cool judgment that followed him throughout his life.

Leaving Denison in 1874, Hall became sergeant-at-arms of the Texas House of Representatives before joining the Ranger force as a first lieutenant. As a Ranger he had no equal in his time. He helped break up the Sutton-Taylor feud and made war on criminals up and down the Mexican border. Fear he knew not. He never sent his men where

106

danger was greatest. That part of the work he assumed himself.

An example of Hall's reckless courage, which contributed to his lasting reputation as a Texas Ranger, occurred when he arrested the Brazell murderers at Clinton, the county seat of DeWitt County. That crime, which was committed on September 18, 1876, rocked the state. The doctor and his son were awakened at their home at midnight. A law-abiding, Christian gentleman, who had given medical attention to both factions in the Taylor-Sutton feud, then raging, he was thought to be without an enemy.

"Old man, get up and come out of there! Come out, old man!" voices in the night had commanded. The doctor and his three sons were led away. Moments later shots rang out. Brazell and his eighteen-year-old son were murdered, but the two small sons escaped by running away. But they had recognized members of the mob.

On Christmas Eve, 1876, the Brazell murderers were holding high carnival in one of their homes in which a wedding was being held, all the men in the house being armed. Joe Sitterlie, one of the culprits, was to be married, and a dance and celebration was taking place in the home of the bride's father, attended by most of the other accused men.

Hall and his men surrounded the house at night; then, after stationing his men at strategic spots, the Captain, unarmed, walked inside among the gay celebrants, told them who he was, who he wanted and why. He allowed three minutes for the women and children to be removed from danger, then he disarmed the men and calmly permitted the festivities to continue while the Rangers stood guard. The next morning the prisoners were marched to jail in Clinton.

Three of the murderers were sentenced to death, but they gained a new lease on life by reversals of the convictions on appeal. Court battles ensued, and delays, venue changes, and technicalities covered a period of twenty-five years. One conviction, in 1899, was finally upheld. But many of the accused had spent months in jails, and thousands of dollars were spent on lawyer fees. All in all, a telling blow had been struck against the feuders and their brazen lawlessness.

Following his retirement, Hall sought a quieter life and found it as manager of the 250,000-acre Dull ranch in LaSalle and McMullen counties. He died March 11, 1911, having added brilliantly to the luster of the Texas Rangers.

Three of the murder charges against Fisher were shifted to Uvalde County on change of venue. Alexander Zimmerman, employer of two of the Mexicans Fisher was charged with killing, though not easy to locate, was finally served with a subpoena. He was supposed to be a star witness for the state. His home was in Frio County, and the sheriff there had reported: "I hereby return attachment for A. Zimmerman. I have been to his home several times, but he is on the dodge and hard to get hold of. I will try to get service by the time your District Court meets."

The two cases against the King for killing the two Mexicans—Escanislado and Pancho—were called for trial in Uvalde on April 21, 1881. Juries were empaneled, and in both instances the defendant was found not guilty.

Various dismissals followed this action. Then on May 16, 1881, on motion of the district attorney, the last two charges against King in Maverick County were dismissed because of insufficient evidence. Every other charge against him in that county had then been dropped—because of insufficient evidence to justify trials.

The new King then proceeded to Laredo, accompanied by his friend, John Robert Baylor, for the last trials—six remaining indictments for horse stealing. He demanded trial and on July 14 was tried and promptly acquitted in three cases. The others were dismissed.

The King was free! The court records were for the first time in six years clear of any charge against the most controversial and notorious figure in the history of southwest Texas. Indicted in twenty-one cases, he could claim at least six jury acquittals, all in counties outside King Fisher Territory. And in each of the others the state confessed the evidence was not sufficient to justify trials.

With a clean slate before him, King Fisher resolved, irrevocably, there is every indication, that never again would he be charged with any offense against the peace and dignity of the state. Future events proved beyond doubt that he was sincere and determined to make good on that resolution.

The King had not been choosy about his associates, and as a wild-riding, reckless, daring young cowboy, often surrounded by a host of dangerous men who followed his leadership, he had been a colorful and dominant figure in the border war that raged along the Río Grande for several blood-splattered years. But there was another side of his life.

He was devoted to his wife and family, enjoyed the ranching business, and was active in several money-making enterprises quite aside from the danger and bold adventure so often associated with his life and times.

The first child born to King and Sarah was named Florence. They were then living on the Pendencia. Later they lived in Eagle Pass for a time. There he had a financial interest in a saloon and also engaged in a livery-stable business in partnership with B. A. Bates. Known as Sunset Livery Stable, its assets included horses, omnibusses, ambulances, buggies, carriages, harness, saddles, bridles, and an assortment of other merchandise.

109

The firm's name was Bates and Fisher, and the business apparently thrived. Later, on January 5, 1883, Fisher sold his interest to his partner.

The second daughter, Eugenia (Ninnie), was born in Eagle Pass. At that point it is reported that King decided to sell his interest in the saloon in which he had made an investment. He commented that it was certainly no credit to the two daughters for it to be known that their father was in the saloon business [Kellogg].

On December 2, 1878, King purchased a ranch from James Vivian, along with a string of cattle identified by fifty-one brands, all recorded at Eagle Pass. The ranch was known as the "C. B. Bruton pasture," and the deed records of the transaction fixes the exact location as having been on the Nueces River "one mile below Manchague crossing thence running west to the forked lake, thence down the lake to the fence of L. Vivian, thence to and along the Espantosa Lake."

As early as 1876 the records reveal that Fisher maintained brands, duly recorded in Maverick County. At the same time at least one dozen different Vivians had recorded brands, and a half dozen Brutons did the same.

John Leakey tells of his father's living on the Nueces in 1879, near the Chimney water hole. There were two houses in the area, the other occupied by King Fisher. After purchasing the Vivian ranch, Fisher moved his family to the new site and set up ranching.

Leakey was trying to retrieve several hundred cattle that had been turned loose in the area by a man named Shackleford, who had either been killed or had left the country. King made a hand for Leakey, acting the part of a good neighbor, in some of the difficult roundups in the thick brush. Mexican bandits were still very active.

"King was a good man on a horse," remembered Leakey, "and a quick one with a rope, in the brush and out. He was also a good man on a trail, Indian or animal, and quick to see and read horse tracks—tracks that might mean anything but often meant danger, sometimes to himself, more often to the men he trailed. There were no railroads in the area southwest of San Antonio at the time King was roaming the range, but he lived to see the coming of the Southern Pacific into Uvalde County in 1884."

The late Reverend Bruce Roberts, a highly respected early-day Baptist missionary preacher, who spent fifty-one years in the Uvalde–Eagle Pass–Carrizo Springs–Laredo area, absorbed much of the King Fisher legend. He was a close friend and neighbor of King's surviving family, and he heard the stories of Fisher's exploits related many times, often at firsthand. He expressed the opinion that many of the charges against Fisher were not true [Roberts, *Springs from the Parched Ground*].

Describing the King as six feet, one inch in height, weight about 185 pounds, Roberts pictured him as of fine physique and manly bearing, gentle, courteous, and thoughtful to others. He quotes Florence, the King's oldest daughter—who was six when her father was killed—as recalling that he always rose to his feet when her mother entered a room where Fisher was seated.

"Almost every person that ever walked out of Fisher's presence did so with a feeling that he would like to say something nice about him," wrote Roberts.

The minister recited an interesting account of King's attending a church service in July, 1882—as related to Roberts by those present. The occasion was an annual four-day meeting of the Río Grande Baptist Association, at Carrizo Springs, attended by people from one dozen south Texas counties. O. C. Pope, superintendent of state missions, was present and delivered a Sunday sermon, Fisher being among those present.

As reported by Roberts, Pope talked that day about the perils of drifting, leading to lawlessness and sin. During lunch hour, the notorious visitor was the center of interest. "Children huddled close to Ma and Pa."

At this point the King drew Pope aside for a talk. Onlookers wondered if he was expressing resentment over something the speaker had said during his sermon.

"What Fisher said to Dr. Pope made a profound impression on the listener, as it did when passed on to me later," said Roberts. We here give Fisher's words from memory, knowing they are not correct word for word. But they are so nearly correct that we prefer to give them as direct quotation:

Dr. Pope, I want to bear testimony to the truth of what you said today. I know how easy it is to drift. I was just a boy, away from home, with poor advantages, but still I had pretty good ideas of what I wanted to be. Then I drifted into bad company, and there didn't seem to be anything much to hold me back from doing wrong. Some of the older people seemed to like me, but it seems they didn't know how to tell me how to go straight. Of course they thought I wouldn't pay any attention to anything they'd say, but I wish they'd tried me out a little more.

Captain McNelly and his Rangers came and took me and some other fellows in. But Captain McNelly gave me some mighty good talk. I've heard that he always carried a little Bible with him. Anyway, it seemed like the Captain was on the right road. It made me think of a preacher I heard once talking about being on the King's highway. I remembered that I said to

112

myself, "King, it would be a lot better for you, if you could be on the King's Highway." I never saw the Captain anymore. He had a cough at that time that sounded bad to me, and sure enough in a little more than a year he was gone. I have wished that I had when we were together that time talked with him about his road, but being a prisoner . . . you know . . . well, I didn't.

Dr. Pope, I have remembered the Captain's talk, and I am going to remember your talk today. I am trying to shape things up to where I can travel a different road.

Roberts recalled that at the next annual session of the same group, which convened at Leakey on July 13, 1883, Pope was again present. He inquired about his friend King Fisher and learned that the repentant King was then chief deputy sheriff of Uvalde County.

The pleasing personality which had so impressed Pope was recognized far and wide. Mrs. Albert Maverick, Sr., who in 1928 wrote about ranch life in Bandera County in 1878, recalled the time she met King Fisher.

One of the most celebrated people we had to visit was King Fisher, at the height of his career. He arrived late one evening with cowboys and a good sized bunch of cattle. Someone explained that he wished to sleep in the house for fear of being killed in the night by some of his various enemies. That night he was careful when he sat at the supper table not to be a target for a gun, but as Rose Kalka, a little Polish girl, happened to touch him while handing around the batter cakes, he jumped like his time had come. He slept in a small room on the gallery.

After all was quiet, I spent a very restless time—and one time when he got up to get a drink of water from

113

the bucket, I held my baby very tight thinking we would die together. I didn't realize that he was a man-killer and not a baby-killer. To my inexperienced eye he was a very innocent looking cowboy, tall, thin and dark. He and I had a very pleasant conversation about his wife and babies before I knew who he was. . . . [Maverick]

During the time King was getting down to serious ranching, he was approached by J. B. Boatright, sheriff of Uvalde County, who asked him to become a deputy. At first Fisher demurred, but the job had an appeal for him. A Ranger, G. K. Chinn, encouraged him to take the job, and Fisher then informed the Sheriff that he would take it, with the understanding that when the election came around in 1884 he would be a candidate for sheriff, to succeed Boatright.

This was in keeping with the King's nature—not to be second in command very long at a time.

King was sworn in as deputy sheriff—in one of the most important counties in southwest Texas at that time. He acquired a home in Uvalde, at 128 Mesquite Street, where the home of Mrs. M. B. Walcott now stands. He and family lived there until his death. A daughter, Mittie, was born there. Another daughter, born November 25, 1881, died on January 2 of the following year.

Sheriff Boatright was soon to get into some personal trouble. An indictment was returned against him on October 1, 1883, and the King took over as acting sheriff.

As a fearless, resourceful peace officer, Fisher stood out during the months following. His had become a well-known name in law enforcement. The Uvalde criminal court records were cluttered at that time with indictments against various members of the Hannehan family, including Mary,

114

the mother. Both James Hannehan and his mother were indicted for murder on April 13, 1880. Killing and stealing were common for members of that notorious family, and they were regarded as dangerous and difficult to subdue. Peace officers were not anxious to tangle with them. Another son, John Hannehan, was indicted at the same time for cattle theft, for which he later was convicted and served two years. And in 1883 Thomas Hannehan was indicted in seven cases. That was while King was deputy.

John Leakey was living in the town of Leakey at the time, forty-five miles from Uvalde. He recalled that his father went down to Uvalde to serve as a deputy under King after Boatright's troubles developed and King had taken over as acting sheriff. Leakey told of the robbing of the San Antonio–El Paso stage, and Fisher hastened to the scene. Two suspects—Tom and Jim Hannehan—were followed to their ranch on the Leona River. They resisted arrest, and during the encounter that followed, King killed Tom, captured Jim, and recovered the loot.

Leakey said that for several years following the death of King Fisher, Mrs. Hannehan, mother of the outlaw son King had killed, made it a practice of coming to the cemetery in Uvalde on each anniversary of her son's death. There she would pile brush on King's grave, set a fire, and then "dance with devilish glee" around the grave as the brush burned.

As the Uvalde deputy got into the swing of the office, his career as a great peace officer was soon well established. He was frequently called upon by neighboring counties to help handle difficult situations that developed in their law enforcement, and he took pride in responding. His greatest attribute was in knowing how to handle and get along with people.

115

My father once told me of an occasion in 1883 when two men, both known to him, were indicted for stealing in Llano County. They went "on the dodge" and soon showed themselves in Uvalde, where they sought help from King— they being indirectly related to him. He lectured them sternly, told them they were following the wrong course, and agreed not to arrest them if they would promise to promptly return to Llano, surrender, and let the law take its course. They agreed and kept their word.

Riding a tide of popularity, King became a candidate for sheriff of Uvalde County early in 1884. The position of sheriff of a county in those days was one of the most honored and respected of any local office. More was expected, and more was required, of a sheriff then than now because the duties were arduous and fraught with constant danger and risk, particularly in southwest Texas. A sheriff's badge was a badge of honor, and his office was one of public esteem and respect, more so than any other local public office.

The election of Fisher became a foregone conclusion. The job was his for the asking, and he took great pride in the confidence he commanded on every hand. Children stared in awe and admiration as he walked the streets, and his worshipers gathered around him wherever he stopped.

XIII
A Fatal Trip

KING FISHER HAD BEEN ACTING SHERIFF at Uvalde for about eight months before fence-cutting business took him to Austin. The invention of barbed wire in 1873 had made it possible for the first time to fence the open ranges. While a godsend for ranchmen, the wire was often a source of headache for peace officers. Once begun, the fencing habit spread rapidly. It was said that seven thousand tons of barbed wire had been sold in Texas by 1877, and the tempo increased after that. Pioneered by John W. ("Bet-a-Million") Gates, the wire found a hungry market. The day of the free range was drawing to a close.

Fence cutting became prevalent in Uvalde and other counties, and since the practice was not then a major crime, little could be done to halt it. Governor John Ireland called the legislature into special session early in 1884 for the purpose of having fence cutting made a felony, so serious had the problem become. The law was enacted but with a provision that gates be installed to enable the small landowners ingress and egress to their homes in case a big pasture was fenced, the outer limits of which encircled them.

After the new law was enacted Fisher, as chief law enforcer in Uvalde County, sought detailed information and instructions on the application of the new statute. The Southern Pacific Railway had completed its link from San

Antonio to Uvalde and westward, and King was able to board a passenger train for Austin. He stopped over in San Antonio, attended some business in the federal court there, and probably some business for a friend who had sent a herd of cattle below San Antonio for sale, and then proceeded to the state capital.

A dispatch to the *Galveston Daily News* from San Antonio, dated March 12, reported that, "Yesterday the representatives of the *News* met King Fisher in the U.S. District Court room and elicited the fact that he was en route as companion to parties who were to visit the Capitol City on business connected with fence-cutters who had assumed a threatening attitude toward county officials, especially in Medina County." Medina County adjoined Uvalde, and the King was evidently going beyond the call of duty in trying to help his neighbors. But his own county was also plagued with fence cutters, and he needed more information concerning the new law.

In Austin the Uvalde official tended to his business, and in the afternoon met with Ben Thompson, former city marshal of Austin and one of the nation's most noted gunslingers. In fact, Bat Masterson, while sheriff at Dodge City, declared Thompson to be the most remarkable man with a pistol he had ever known. To use the marshal's own words: "It is doubtful whether, in his time, there was another man living who equaled him with a pistol in a life and death struggle."

A native of England, Thompson was born November 11, 1842. He was described as five feet, nine inches in height, rather swarthy in complexion, stoutly built, with black hair and blue eyes. Ben was quick in all his motions, possessed indomitable energy, and was as fearless as a lion. He was said by his biographer, Major William M. Walton, to have been a generous man, the friend of the weak and oppressed, and one whose loyalty to his friends knew no bounds.

He always fought clean and had no respect for a man who sought an unfair advantage in a fight. When unarmed or a noncombatant, a man was always safe in his presence. And that included his enemies.

Ben had been in a bad mood when he chanced to meet Fisher on the streets of Austin that day. Their prior relationship is not known, but it is assumed that they knew each other, and they appeared to be on friendly terms. The press at the time described them as friends. And so did Ben's biographers.

Thompson had killed Jack Harris in the Vaudeville gambling house in San Antonio twenty months earlier, for which he was acquitted by a San Antonio jury. Following that episode, Ben had resigned as city marshal of Austin, to which position he had been previously elected.

After the murder trial, Thompson became irritable and began drinking heavily. He became involved in many minor gun plays, always having his way. In fact, it got to the point where each morning Austin residents could be heard to ask: "What did Ben Thompson do last night?"

The killing of Jack Harris in 1882 precipitated the tragedy that befell Thompson and Fisher in San Antonio on the night of the day they met in Austin. Therefore, the circumstances of that prior encounter become relevant [Walton, Streeter].

Harris operated the Vaudeville Variety Theater, where there was legalized gambling, and was its principal owner. The Vaudeville, along with the Silver Dollar Saloon and the White Elephant, were leading places in San Antonio at the time for gamblers and fun seekers to hang out. The Harris place was located on Main Plaza and Soledad streets, where the National Bank of Commerce now stands. In fact, it became known as the Fatal Corner because of the regularity of shootings that were staged there. At least six killings had been recorded there, including the killing of Harris. It was in the old Vaudeville that the beautiful Georgia Lake was slain and a young man blew his brains out with a pistol.

The Vaudeville was a combination gambling house, saloon, and variety theater that featured scantily clad girls and stock-company entertainment of varied quality. With a bevy of attractive song-and-dance girls, the bill of performance included Irish and Dutch comedians, magicians, gymnasts, and club swingers.

The place was said to have been the most widely advertised resort in western Texas. Housed in a two-story building, its saloon was in the front part of the ground floor, with a theater in the rear. The gambling hall was upstairs, with a theater balcony, under which was Sim Hart's Cigar Store. The front pavement was covered by an extended gallery roof. Two doors, some twelve feet apart, marked the entrance. A crescent-shaped bar graced the saloon, some twenty feet inside from the street. Between the bar and the front doors was a screen made of venetian blinds, with swinging doors, which crossed the room for ingress and egress to the bar.

Opened in 1879, the Vaudeville went up in flames on the morning of March 3, 1886. The institution's demise was described in the *San Antonio Express*: "Thus perished the walls that once resounded to the husky songs of threadbare divas, the guffaws of cowboys out for an evening, the rattle of dice and the roar of gunfire."

San Antonio at the time was busy and full of excitement. One writer said "cattle, wool, faro, good air, and swift horses had brought plenty of wealth to the Alamo City;

that ranchmen played at crack-loo on its cobbled sidewalks with double eagles, and gamblers backed their choice of a card with stacks of chips limited solely by the law of gravity."

Associated with Harris in the theater were Joe Foster, a small, frail man, and William H. (Billy) Simms, a native of Austin. Before coming to San Antonio, Simms had known Ben Thompson at the state capital. They had worked together as "devils" in an Austin printing shop as boys, but later when they were operating gambling houses in Austin, some animosity had arisen between them.

Foster, a native of Missouri, had answered the call of the California gold rush and had served in the Confederate Army. After the war he had chosen San Antonio for his home, later buying an interest in the Variety, then a lucrative business. He was a gambler, immaculate in dress, dignified in appearance, abstemious in habits, cold-eyed, and himself quick on the draw.

Prior to the Thompson-Harris encounter, Ben had sat in a faro game in the Harris place, with Joe Foster. The latter did the dealing, Thompson the betting. A controversy arose. One version is that Ben lost money, then put some diamonds into the game, agreeing to redeem them, and later decided the game was crooked, denounced Foster as a swindler, drew his pistol, then backed out of the room.

When this incident was reported to Harris, he made it plain that Thompson would not be welcome to enter his place again. And that word was relayed to Ben.

Early in 1882, some two years later, Thompson, then city marshal of Austin, had business in San Antonio. During the evening, he learned that Harris had been seen on the street with a shotgun, probably looking for him. The next morning they met, and Ben said:

"Hello, Jack! I understand that you were on the hunt for me last night with your shotgun, is that so?"

"No," replied Harris, "I was not looking for you, but I was waiting for you and if you had come about my place I would have filled you full of shot."

The intervention of a deputy sheriff, Señor Penolosa, probably prevented an encounter as tempers flared. Thompson continued:

> I understand you and your crew are forted for me and intend to shoot me, if you can get the advantage— now let me tell you, go and get your crew of assassins, arm them with shotguns and Winchester rifles, and come out on the Main Plaza, and I will run all of you to your holes; come out and fight like men. . . .

Billy Simms, sensing trouble, had brought two pistols to the Vaudeville. The air was filled with tenseness when later on Thompson made a call at the gambling house. He had a friend there named "Bones" who kept one of the gambling tables, and when they met Bones reacted in a way that alerted the wiley Ben to the imminence of trouble. Thompson drew his pistol and backed out of the door. As the day wore on Ben did some drinking and was preparing to go out to San Pedro Springs with some friends for supper. His hack was late, and the Austin marshal gravitated down to the Vaudeville again. He went in with two friends, Charlie Bennett and Dick Strayhorn, called for a drink, and said to the bartender:

"Where's that shotgun brigade that is on the hunt for me?"

Barney Mitchell, the bar keeper, denied knowing of such a brigade.

"You tell Joe Foster he is a thief, and tell Jack Harris he is living off the labors of these poor variety women."

The drink mixer replied: ". . . If you want such word conveyed to them, you can tell them yourself."

Thompson and his friends walked out. The gunman's appearance in the bar had created quite a stir. Harris was sent for; Simms went upstairs and got the two pistols, then walked down the sidewalk to intercept Harris.

Ben re-entered and again asked the bartender why the shotgun brigade did not show up and said he intended to close up the house. As he left, Harris, unseen by Thompson, entered through another door.

Outside, Ben met Simms and they chatted. Simms later claimed he urged the marshal not to raise a disturbance, and was told: "There's going to be hell here tonight. There is no use talking to me, Billy." When they parted, Ben paced up and down the sidewalk, then stood near the curb facing the saloon, his arms folded. Inside, Harris had readied his shotgun, and he took a position near the ticket office behind a set-off in the doorway that led up the stairway. From this vantage point he could see through the Venetian screen and out into the street, thus giving him what he thought was the advantage he needed.

As he stood in front, Thompson overheard some one who was leaving remark: "Jack has got his gun." This prompted Ben to close in and peer through the blinds.

"What are you doing with that gun?" he was quoted as asking.

"To shoot you, you damned s——o——b——!" Harris retorted.

"Come on, I'm ready for you," said Harris, evidently thinking he had the drop and could raise the gun and fire in plenty of time. But he made a fatal miscalculation. The veteran gunman went into action. In a flash he whipped his pistol out and thumbed its hammer so fast its three shots sounded like one. Firing through the latticed screen, Ben's first shot, which was fatal, ricocheted and struck along the top of the wainscotting against the wall just as Harris raised the shotgun. The victim died later that evening.

The funeral the next day was described as a more affecting spectacle than anything ever seen in the theater which the deceased had operated. While his dog, Skeezicks, stood guard by the hearse, women from the Vaudeville were said to have wept copiously over the flower-strewn grave. A prominent San Antonio minister officiated at a dramatic burial service.

On the Vaudeville's ledger, containing a log of performers each day, and comments, is found the following notation: "July 11—Jack Harris, proprietor, shot and killed by Ben Thompson at 7:15 P.M. Died as he lived, a true friend and a kind-hearted, generous gentleman. 'God have mercy on his soul.' "

The next notation, dated July 15, states: "House reopened under the management of Simms, Foster, and Dyer (for the estate). Company contracts as before. But the Old House ain't like it used to be."

After the shooting Thompson hurried away and spent the night at the Menger Hotel. The following day he sent for the sheriff and city marshal, surrendered, and was locked up in the Bat Cave—the same jail King Fisher had spent time in four years before.

Thompson was indicted, and the famous murder trial which followed, beginning January 16, 1882, attracted the best legal talent in the state. Major T. T. Teel was employed as a special prosecutor. Also connected with the case were

124

Judge Thomas J. Ervine, the law firms of Tarleton & Boone and Anderson & Anderson, district attorney Wallace from an adjoining district, and Fred Cocke, state's attorney.

Major W. M. (Buck) Walton headed the array of defense counsel. Others included John A. and N. O. Green, of the San Antonio bar. John Green had been a life-long friend of Thompson's. In addition, there were Sheeks & Sneed and Wooten & Poindexter, of Austin, and J. Minor, of San Antonio.

Walton, the leading defense counsel, of Austin, had served as attorney general of Texas. Walton was a personal friend of Thompson's and was engaged in the writing of his biography at the time Thompson was killed.

Judge G. H. Noonan presided at the trial, held in the Old Courthouse on Soledad Street. Before a packed room, the trial proceeded. After testimony was completed, the lawyers put everything they had into their summations. Leo Tarleton opened for the state, T. T. Teel closed for the state, and W. M. Walton made the concluding argument for the defense.

When a not-guilty verdict was returned, a noisy demonstration by Thompson's friends took place in the courtroom. Ben's return to Austin sparked one of the most remarkable demonstrations on Congress Avenue in that city's history.

While the acquittal was widely acclaimed, the incident completely changed the course of Ben Thompson's life. He was never quite the same after that. He was less attentive to his dress, drank excessively, and was given to insomnia and brooding. His mother died, and his brother had been beset with troubles. He became increasingly irritable, would fire his pistol into the air, and on one occasion used it to make a bartender serve some Negroes at a bar reserved for whites. For this outburst he later apologized, then went out and fired a half dozen shots into an organ which an itinerant organ grinder kept on a street corner. The next day he was back to apologize and pay for the damages.

Ben became insulting and overbearing toward people for whom he had no reason to harbor animosity. In a spirit of deviltry and with nothing better to do, he "staggered" into a theater, appeared in a box, and putting on a drunk act called out for liquor, then commenced firing his gun promiscuously into the crowd. In no time he was alone in the hall. It was his way of having a little fun. The shells he fired were all blank!

It was shortly after this that King chanced to meet up with Ben on March 11, 1884. Ben presented him with a photograph of himself, and they visited around the capital city.

Some time before, according to Major W. M. Walton, who wrote the book, *The Life of Ben Thompson*, Fisher and Thompson had become angered at each other, but through the intervention of friends there was a very hearty reconciliation. It was said King had resented the killing of Jack Harris, with whom he had been on cordial terms. Thompson was probably not very happy over the fact that T. T. Teel, who had been King's lawyer for years, was employed to prosecute him and probably pled the state's case in a manner not too pleasing to Thompson.

After visiting in Austin, Fisher was to depart by train for Uvalde, via San Antonio. It is not clear at whose instance Ben decided to make the trip south with his friend. They reached the train as it was moving off, commandeered a carriage, and drove rapidly to the bridge across the Colorado River to a point where the trains slow up, and there they were able to board. Thompson was drinking and apparently had no plans to revisit the Vaudeville. In fact, he had been quoted as saying Joe Foster had invited him back to the theater, "but they do not catch me in that trap. I know if I were to go into that place it would be my graveyard."

It was also reported that Ben first decided to go with Fisher out to where the outgoing train met an incoming one and switch trains there. But once he was on board he did not want to leave the company of Uvalde's acting sheriff. Thompson's drinking continued, and he pulled pranks by taking a bottle of whisky away from a passenger, then proceeding to strike the colored porter with the bottle when he did not respond to one of Ben's requests. That incident prompted Fisher bluntly to tell Ben to cut it out.

Someone sent a telegram from one of the train stops, warning the people in San Antonio that Thompson, accompanied by King, was on his way there. Simms is said to have shown the telegram to the city marshal and also to a local judge. The latter advised him to arm himself with a shotgun. Simms allegedly conferred with Joe Foster and also with Jacob Coy, a half-Mexican, who was a special policeman who worked at the theater as a sort of special officer or "bouncer." It was said that the police instructed those who encountered Ben to kill him upon the slightest provocation. The stage was set for some serious trouble once Ben arrived on the scene.

Arriving in San Antonio about eight o'clock that evening, the two men proceeded to the Turner Hall Opera House at Houston and St. Mary's streets, where the Brady building now stands. There they saw Ada Gray playing in *Lady Audley's Secret*, which had been presented in the Austin Opera House the night before. Ben wanted to see the performance again.

After the show they stopped in at Gallagher's Saloon, and while there Ben told about his encounter with the porter on the train and how he came to cut a part out of the crown on his hat. Still drinking, he had visited the bar at intervals during the show at Turner's.

Years later Tom Vanderhaven, a San Antonio attorney, who was a personal friend of King Fisher, told Terrell Kellogg, the King's grandson, that he had warned King of the possibility of tragedy that evening if he remained with Thompson. He even suggested that his colored driver take King in the attorney's hack and remove him from the danger area. But Fisher apparently did not share his friend's concern. He evidently felt that he could handle the situation and avoid trouble.

Thompson and Fisher boarded a hack and proceeded to the Vaudeville, then being operated by Joe Foster and Billy Simms, who had taken over after Harris' death.

They first stopped at the bar downstairs, where Thompson had a drink. Then they went upstairs where a variety show was in progress. Here they were seated and served drinks by girls in short skirts and red stockings. One version has it that Simms invited the girls upstairs.

Upon the two men's arrival, Jacob Coy reported to Deputy Marshal Corbet, in the building at the time, that King Fisher had just come in and was armed. Coy was not supposed to admit guests who carried guns. The officer assured him that Fisher, being an officer, had a legal right to wear the gun.

The time was about ten-thirty in the evening. Upstairs, Ben had another drink, and King called for a cigar. Special Officer Coy joined them, and Thompson allegedly began talking about the Jack Harris killing. There was some shifting of seats, and King was quoted as saying he thought they had dropped in to have fun and not to talk about unpleasant subjects. He, probably sensing trouble, suggested they go

128

downstairs, and they all arose and moved toward the doorway leading down. At that point Joe Foster joined them. Ben had seen him nearby and asked: "Billy, ain't that Joe Foster over there?" Foster was asked to join them, and Thompson offered to shake hands and have a drink. But Foster bluntly refused to do either.

There was an exchange of unpleasant talk between them, with Ben showing signs of anger. Foster, Simms, and Coy all claimed Thompson pulled his gun and struck Foster in the mouth with it, and that Coy grabbed the barrel as it fired. They insisted Thompson kept firing, four or five times, and that one shot struck Foster in the leg; that other shooting then followed, after the first two shots; that Thompson, Fisher, and Coy all went down in a heap, Coy still clutching the barrel of Thompson's gun. This was the version given by Simms and his confederates.

A witness who reached the scene of the tragedy a few moments after the killing reported that the two bodies were weltering in blood, laid out side by side, their hair and faces carmined with the life fluid. The stairs leading up to the scene of horror (Foster had been carried down them), were as slippery as ice, the walls were stained, and the floor was tracked with bloody foot prints. Dissolute women with blanched faces, he added, crowded around with exclamations and broken sobs, exclaiming: "Which is Ben?" "Show me Ben!" "Is that him?" Even in his death, amid the garish surroundings, the grim reputation of the man who was best known at the Vaudeville, stood forth as strong as ever.

Thompson and Fisher were dead. Foster had a leg wound which proved fatal. Coy suffered a slight flesh wound. Pandemonium followed, with women dragging their skirts through the bloody gore as they tried to get a glance at the dead men.

129

As the bodies lay in silent death, Thompson's expression, it was said, was stern, the upper lip drawn taut across his teeth, his waxed mustache curling upward, and his gray eyes set in a ghastly stare.

The picture which Ben had given King was found in the latter's pocket. One of Fisher's arms lay across his companion's body, as though, according to Thompson's admirers, even in death to insist on defending his friend, while the King wore "a pallid and peaceful expression," his pistol in its holster, undrawn and unfired.

An Austin newspaper in a banner headline reported: BEN THOMPSON, HERO OF MANY A BLOODY FIGHT, HAS FOUGHT HIS LAST AND DIED LAST NIGHT. KING FISHER, FAITHFUL TO THE END, YIELDED UP HIS LIFE TO SAVE A FRIEND.

The version of the killing given by Simms, Foster, and Coy, recounted above, was hotly disputed by other eyewitnesses to the tragedy. Simms testified at the coroner's hearing that Thompson "drew his six-shooter and struck it sideways in Foster's mouth and cocked it as he pulled it back from Foster's mouth," whereupon Foster swung at Ben with his fists, then drew his pistol. Coy grabbed Ben's gun by the cylinder and a scuffle ensued, according to the witness. They all contended Simms drew just as Foster flew into Ben, then all began firing simultaneously.

The bodies were taken by the undertakers, Carter and Mullaly, to the Bat Cave, which also served as police headquarters at the time, where the dead men were temporarily laid out, after being viewed at the scene of the shooting by a hastily summoned coroner's jury.

By a coincidence Foster was moved to the house occupied by Jack Harris when he died from Ben Thompson's bullet

130

nearly two years before. Foster died there on March 22.

Exactly one week after the tragedy, a reporter for the *San Antonio Express* interviewed Foster at his room, and the latter said he shot Thompson in the chest during the struggle. Foster added that after he, Fisher, and Coy fell, he held his pistol to Thompson's left eye and fired again, and followed that with four shots fired "into the crowd," meaning the men who had fallen. The autopsy, however, did not disclose a breast wound, as claimed by Foster.

The coroner's report stated that Ben received four shots, two of which would have produced instant death. Thompson was shot just over the left eye, in the left temple, in the breast, and in the abdomen. King was hit in the left eye, in the breast just below the heart, and in the right leg. Both men had powder burns about their faces.

The coroner's jury of six reassembled the morning following the shooting. It was made up of George Hilgers, M. L. Ansell, J. A. Bennett, E. J. Gaston, J. M. Martin, and R. W. Wallace. The hearing was held in the office of Anton Adam, a justice of the peace.

Justice Adam's office was in a small adobe room on Verimendi Street, between Soledad Street and Main Avenue, to the rear of the baking house operated by Leonardo Garza, site of the present Wolff & Marx Department Store. Six witnesses were heard: Constable Casanovas, Jacob Coy, Officer Chadwell, City Marshal Phil Shardein, J. J. Emerson, and Billy Simms. Chadwell, who heard the shots from the street, thought he heard eight or nine shots, "fired rapidly." Coy thought there were twelve or thirteen.

It took the jury ten minutes to return a verdict finding that the two men came to their deaths from the "effect of pistol shot wounds from pistols held in and fired from the hands of J. C. Foster and Jacob Coy, and we further find that the said killing was justifiable and done in self defense in the immediate danger of life."

Few shooting incidents in Texas have attracted so much attention. The tragedy was headlined in every daily in the state and in some other states. In an editorial published in Austin three days after the killing it was estimated that no less than ten thousand columns of space had carried the story. Years later J. F. Marshall, of San Antonio, who was a Western Union telegrapher on the fatal night, recalled the rush for the wire services. He had received a call at home: "Come to the office at once. Ben Thompson has been killed."

Western Union's five operators were all called in. They worked through three days and nights, stopping only long enough to catch short naps. Meals were brought to them.

A Galveston reporter breezed in after the shooting, Marshall recalled, picked up a big dictionary, and ordered: "Send this to my paper. . . ." This was his way of tying up the line ahead of other reporters. As the telegrapher sent out hundreds of meaningless words from the dictionary, the reporter composed his story, a long one, which was then sent on its way. Marshall retained the dictionary as a souvenir, and went to the Bat Cave and viewed the bodies the next day.

The press reported that news of the killings spread instantly in the city that night and that an estimated four thousand people gathered around the Vaudeville, seeking a chance to see the bodies.

"The dead men," said the reporter for the *Galveston News*, "met their fate side by side, in a corner formed by the partition wall separating the saloon from the auditorium, and the wall of a private box to the right of the entrance to

132

the dress circle. With the firing of the first shot the circle was cleared, the occupants jumping into the marquette below and through the side windows and into the streets. . . . The news spread with remarkable rapidity. . . ."

The coroner's jury verdict was widely criticized. It had featured the version of interested witnesses—those who had participated and could be expected to be self-serving and biased. There was strong belief, supported by physical facts and by at least two disinterested eyewitnesses, that Fisher and Thompson went upstairs at the Vaudeville that night at the suggestion of Billy Simms, and that an ambush was awaiting them there.

XIV

Eyewitnesses Confirm Ambush

AN *Austin Statesman* reporter interviewed two witnesses, both salesmen, one from Chicago and the other from Kentucky. They said they were taken by a San Antonio businessman friend on an evening sight-seeing tour, including a stop at the Vaudeville. They were in the barroom when Thompson and Fisher came in, and the friend pointed out the notorious Ben Thompson who had killed Harris in that room where they were standing.

A man identified as Simms approached the gunmen, shook hands, and Thompson, in their hearing, assured Simms he wanted to bury the hatchet and be friends. Then Simms invited them upstairs to see Foster.

These two men, identified as Alex T. Raymond and John R. Sublett, entranced by curiosity, followed the noted visitors upstairs and took nearby seats to observe them and listen. They emphasized that Simms appeared very friendly. As they recalled it, the conversation went like this, before they proceeded upstairs:

"Ben, I am awful glad to see you here. Let us forget the past, and be friends in the future."

Thompson: "I desire to be friends, and I have come here with my friend Fisher to talk the matter over, and have a perfect understanding. I have a perfect right to do that, have I not?"

"Yes, Ben," replied Simms, "That is right, and I know we can all be friends."

Then Ben added: "I have nothing against you or Foster. I am not afraid of you. I am here surrounded by my friends. . . ."

Upstairs, according to these witnesses, the three were soon joined by Coy, who sat down with them, and there was pleasant conversation. Ben ordered drinks, teased about paying, then pulled out a roll, saying "I have lots of money. I have $20,000 in that roll! . . . I thought you brought me up here to see Foster. Billy, don't you play any games on me. I did not come here for any fuss, and I don't want any, but you must treat me fair."

Then Simms said he would find Foster so there could be friendly talk.

At that point Fisher broke in: "Yes, go and get him. I want to make you fellows good friends before I leave. I have invited Thompson here; he did not want to come, but you are all friends of mine, and I want you to be friends. I told him to come and talk the matter over like gentlemen together, and bury the past; Thompson is willing to do it, and I want Foster to meet him half way."

Then Simms said he would go and get Foster.

Foster was brought over, and as he approached Ben, without rising, extended his hand to Foster, and as he did, King explained:

"I want you and Thompson to be friends. You are both friends to me, and I want you to shake hands like gentlemen."

Foster replied: "I cannot shake hands with Ben Thompson, nor can I be friends, and I want him to keep out of my way!"

The witnesses reported that both Simms and Coy then

stepped to one side, at least two feet from where Thompson and Fisher were sitting, and Foster was about the same distance on the other side of them. Both Ben and King sprang to their feet, neither with a pistol in his hand, and before they got to their feet a volley that sounded like a dozen carbines was fired from a box a little to the left and considerably above the doomed men, and both went down instantly.

Neither of the victims drew his gun, and neither had time to do so. Any statement to the contrary was without the slightest foundation, according to Raymond and Sublett. Both victims fell when the volley was fired; then either Simms or Coy rushed up and drew Thompson's pistol and bent over, putting the muzzle close to the dead man's ear, and fired. He then fired two more shots into his head and body and the other man shot Fisher in a similar manner. Foster, they said, tried to draw his revolver, but it caught and he gave it an angry jerk bringing it out. The jerk discharged it and the ball struck him in the leg and he fell. The crowd then gathered around the dead men.

"It's monstrous," said Mr. Raymond.

This version was published, and the witnesses were then available had a grand jury chosen to question and cross examine them under oath. There is no indication, however, that was done. On the contrary, it appears that San Antonio authorities blinked their eyes at these accounts and were quite content to accept the coroner's verdict. The grand jury returned no indictments.

The inaction of San Antonio authorities aroused strong feeling in Austin. The day after the shooting, the *Statesman*'s San Antonio reporter, commenting on the confusion and inaction of officers, said: "Had such an occurrence taken place in Austin, and the police failed to make an arrest, I suspect your city administration would be subjected to rather severe criticism."

Accenting the muddle, the same reporter, after the coroner's verdict, said: "It is believed that Thompson was killed by his own pistol, in the hands of Coy. Coy's pistol was fully loaded and Fisher's was found in the scabbard. . . . He [Fisher] was personally popular in the West, and his death will be regretted by many. It is the irony of fate that men with the reputation for personal prowess possessed by the departed should be shot like dogs and butchered like sheep in the shambles, without one life in exchange for their own."

Continuing Austin's outburst of indignation, the *Daily Dispatch* blasted: ". . . There never was, and we trust there never will be, such a cowardly and brutal act committed in our city. San Antonio is alone in this great country where hired assassination is endured and approved by the people and the press and it is welcome to the glory."

In Austin the coroner's verdict was treated as a cover-up. "Foul murder," "slaughter," and "cowardly assassination," were the appellations used to describe the episode. The *Daily Capitol* in its March 15 issue joined in the conviction that a successful ambush had been pulled.

"It is not the death of Ben Thompson," the paper said, "that occasions so much indignation in Austin, and among honorable men everywhere who know anything of the circumstances, but it was the manner, the 'deep damnation of his taking off,' that galls. . . ."

Still another man, Thomas McGee, a north Texas stockman, was seated in the balcony and was also an eyewitness. He agreed that as he saw it neither Thompson nor Fisher

137

drew his pistol. In fact, Andreas Coy, a brother of the special policeman, was quoted in the press as saying he did not believe that Ben fired a shot.

All these disinterested witnesses agreed that Ben was in a jovial mood that night; that he asked the group what they wanted to drink; that two cigars, a glass of beer, and one whisky and seltzer were ordered. Fisher was a cigar smoker.

Moreover, it is considered doubtful that Joe Foster would have employed the provocative language he was quoted as using had he not known that Thompson was covered. To have acted as he did in the absence of such knowledge would, to say the least, have been the act of a very foolish man not afraid to die. While his refusal to shake hands and have a drink might not have incited Ben to murder, he ran a definite risk, particularly in view of Thompson's drinking and Foster's offensive greeting. It would seem that his conduct was deliberate, calculated to cause the doomed men to rise to their feet.

But the strongest corroboration of the eyewitness accounts came from the autopsy upon Thompson's body in Austin by Doctors Worthington and Wooten, both reputable medical men. The autopsy was held in the presence of the press and others. Evidently determined to expose the superficiality of the coroner's verdict, Austin authorities were eager to remove any doubt in the public mind about the erroneous character of the findings at the inquest.

Whereas it was said at the inquest that Ben was struck four times, the autopsy found that eight bullets entered his body, five in his head. All eight entered the body on the left side; neither the back, front, nor the right side being hit at all. This strongly indicated that all shots, or most of them, came from the same place. Four of the balls were found to range slightly downward, following about the

138

same angle or course. This finding served to confirm the version given by the eyewitnesses. Some of the bullets were recovered from the body, and were examined by ballistics expert J. C. Petmecky. He found they came from Winchester rifle and .44 cartridges.

Apparently none of this significant evidence was sought or received by the San Antonio grand jury which investigated the tragedy.

An autopsy was not performed on Fisher's body. Testimony heard at the coroner's inquest reported three shots, two of which would have been fatal. But Charles M. Barnes, then a reporter for the *San Antonio Express*, acted as clerk for the coroner and wrote the first day's story for his paper. Barnes reported that the total number of wounds on the two men numbered between twenty-two and twenty-four, some of them by buckshot.

Fisher's gun was never drawn or fired. Thompson's pistol was alleged to contain five empty shells. This adds to the mystery and tends to corroborate Raymond and Sublett. Indeed, one would be quite irrational to contend that Thompson could have fired his pistol five times, yet the gun undoubtedly contained five empty shells.

King's gun, a .45 Colt which had been given to him by Porfirio Díaz, was described in the press as having a black gutta-percha handle and blue-bronze steel cylinder and barrel. It was removed from his body by Officer Chadwell. Thompson's .45 Colt was taken by Coy and turned over to Shardein.

Thus, an analysis of the physical facts and evidence tends to prove very convincingly that Thompson and Fisher were assassinated. It seems utterly incredible that two of the fastest and most deadly gunmen in Texas could be killed in the manner described by Simms, Coy, and Foster.

Thompson's rating as a gunman in Texas was second to none; and Fisher, according to author Eugene Cunningham, "in the border country along the Río Grande, had a name for desperate gunplay, greater even than Thompson's gun."

XV

Assassins Identified

ONE REPORT which has been widely circulated has it that the dirty work was done from a curtained theater box by three hired assassins—a bartender, a gambler, and a performer, all of whom left the city immediately.

George Durham, who as a Ranger was in and out of San Antonio and was rated highly as an officer and detective, was quoted as saying:

> Before I leave the subject of King Fisher, I would like to set the record straight on his death. I am not bragging when I say that I was in a position to know the facts. King Fisher was assassinated by paid killers. I know exactly how much they got. Them assassins was paid to get Ben Thompson. They didn't want King. But King stuck by Ben as he always stuck by a friend; and King was killed.
>
> Billy Simms, credited with the killing, wouldn't have lasted one small fraction of a second before King Fisher. If King Fisher had dreamed he was walking into a death trap that night in Jack Harris' gambling hall, I'll leave it to every man that ever saw King Fisher in action, that he would have cleaned that gambling hall from top to bottom while the others were reaching for their guns. It was an ambush—a $200 ambush.

Fisher was admittedly an innocent victim. He just happened to be with the wrong man at the wrong time at the wrong place. He was on friendly terms with both Simms and Foster. The latter, at his own expense, had carried food and other items to him during his stay in the old Bat Cave six years before, and was quite fond of King. After the Vaudeville tragedy, the press reported that Foster "while under the influence of opiates speaks continuously of King Fisher in the most affectionate terms."

Durham's version was confirmed by Frank H. Bushick, for eight years editor of the *San Antonio Express.* Years later he wrote that he had been told by sporting men who should have known, that three men were stationed in the theater box, armed with Winchester rifles, with instructions to fire in case trouble arose. The three killers were reported to have been a bartender named McLaughlin, a gambler who was known as Canada Bill, and a Jewish performer named Harry Tremaine. They were able to slip out of the theater and promptly left town, he said.

Bushick described the coroner's inquest as perfunctory. Local politics, plus the influence of the gambling fraternity in San Antonio at the time, was given as the best explanation for the failure to seriously investigate and explore the facts at the time.

Thompson's body was claimed by his brother Bill. The latter was at the palatial White Elephant Saloon and gambling hall, only three doors west of the Vaudeville, when the shooting occurred. When he rushed into the street he was met by police with shotguns and warned to be quiet and peaceable.

The Thompson funeral took place in Austin on March 13, under auspices of Mount Bonnell Lodge Number 34, Knights of Pythias, of which Thompson had been a member for many years. Services were held at the Thompson home, with Reverend R. K. Smoot, Presbyterian pastor, officiating. There was an overflow crowd. Bedecked profusely with flowers, the casket was taken in a hearse to the cemetery, preceded by a cortege of sixty-two vehicles, with Thompson's fellow Knights in full dress marching on either side. One carriage contained orphans who were being reared at the expense of the deceased. At the graveside in Oakwood Cemetery fraternal services were read by R. B. Underwood, vice chancellor of the Mount Bonnell Lodge.

Walton, in his biography of Thompson, estimated that he left property worth $10,000. His home, located on the southeast corner of University Avenue at 21st Street, was later sold to E. C. Bartholomew for $5,000, of which $2,000 was paid to Catherine, the widow, "said allowance being in lieu of homestead," and the balance applied on debts. The lot where the Thompson home stood is now the property of the University Christian Church, and on the same property is now located a stone building which houses the Texas Bible Chair.

XVI

King Fisher Mourned

NOW FOR A FINAL WORD about King Fisher. His widow and three small daughters were overcome with grief. The body was taken on the 6:40 P.M. Sunset train by Deputy U.S. Marshal Ferd Niggli, a friend of the deceased. Niggli and other friends accompanied the body on its last ride. The Deputy Marshal had taken charge at the request of the widow. A dispatch from Uvalde, published in the *San Antonio Express*, described the funeral as the biggest one ever held in Uvalde. The Reverend J. W. Stovall was the minister in charge.

The body was interred in a tear-shaped casket, and later a cast-iron fence was erected around the grave. In 1959 the old cemetery was changed to another location, and all the bodies buried there were removed, including that of King Fisher. The casket was opened, and despite the intervention of seventy-five years the body was found to be in an excellent state of preservation. The brass handles on the sides of the coffin were still intact and useable. Final resting place is on the east side of what is now known as Frontier Cemetery.

The King was survived by the widow and the three girls—Florence, who later married Frank Kellogg; Mittie, who married Edgar Campbell; and Ninnie, who married B. F.

McDonald. The last two daughters and their families moved to Imperial Valley in California shortly after marriage. Florence remained at Carrizo Springs and reared three children, all prominent and highly respected.

Although the widow was left with some property, it was of limited value at that time. Her financial problem was somewhat alleviated by contributions from some of King's friends and admirers, which aided in the education of her daughters.

In a *San Antonio Express* story, March 14, a reporter said that the previous morning he had met a gentleman, a resident of Uvalde, who had just arrived on the morning train from there. The Uvaldean, a Fisher family neighbor, said that almost the entire population of that town had gone out to the railway station, one mile north of town, to meet the train bringing the remains of the dead man. The body was escorted to the Fisher residence, where it remained until the funeral on the following afternoon, March 13.

The visitor reported that the death created considerable comment and enlisted deep sympathy, as Fisher's career since he had been in Uvalde had been irreproachable; he was held in high esteem there.

Fisher's record as an officer was good, said the informant, "and he was temperate in his habits, and very quiet and peaceable. The belief there is current that Fisher did not enter into the difficulty intentionally and that he would have averted the trouble which resulted in his death; the people regard it as being a very unfortunate circumstance that he was in Thompson's company on that occasion."

The neighbor added that Fisher's widow was deeply afflicted over the tragedy. He said the shock had been a dreadful one to her nervous system.

145

"He was an exemplary and affectionate husband and father and the close of his career was a consummation hard to be realized. . . ."

It is of particular interest to note a story that appeared in the same paper on March 15, from Uvalde. It cited a communication signed by 271 citizens, including the names of those whom the *Express* editor described as the most prominent people of the community.

The communication took issue with an *Express* story about the shooting in which Fisher was referred to in a disparaging manner. The Uvaldeans began by saying they did not care to discuss the early life of King Fisher but would speak of him as they had known him in their county during the two and one-half years he had lived there. They described him as "kind, courteous, affable, generous, always ready to ferret out crime and bring the criminals to justice.

"And," the statement continued, "he has been the means of bringing to justice some of as bad criminals as ever infested Texas. . . . We feel that we do not exaggerate when we assert that King Fisher has accomplished as much for law and order within the last two and one-half years as any man in Western Texas, and this assertion will be verified by all officers who may have been thrown in contact with him. In justice to the dead and in justice to his family, we ask that this correction be made."

The King was dead. Long live the King! In memory and in legend the life and deeds of this remarkable man continue to live.

As a youngster still in his teens he had shown almost unbelievable leadership qualities, and he had achieved dominance in a crime-infested area. Never as bad as he was pictured, Fisher later switched his allegiance to the side of the law, and in two years of law-enforcement work he achieved fame and distinction as a peace officer.

Now the curtain falls on the thirty-one years lived by King Fisher. Despite what may be said of him, he was not simple. He lived a life of contrasts, jammed full of action, sparked by a magnetic, truly remarkable personality—and he was in the fullest sense part and parcel of the wildest frontier in American history.

Bibliography

Bonnet, W. A. "King Fisher—a Noted Character," *Frontier Times* (July, 1945).

Bushick, Frank H. *Glamorous Days*. Naylor Co., San Antonio, 1934.

Durham, George (As told to Clyde Wantland). "On the Trail of 5,100 Outlaws—Beyond the Nueces," *Valley Morning Star*, Harlingen, Texas, Nov. 8, 1959.

————. *Taming the Nueces Strip*. University of Texas Press, Austin, 1962.

Fisher, Jobe. "*Memoirs*," unpublished, in possession of author, 1937.

Fisher, O. C. *Texas Heritage of the Fishers and the Clarks*. Anson Jones Press, 1963.

Jennings, N. A. *A Texas Ranger*. Scribners, New York, 1899.

Kellogg, Florence. "Incidents in the Life of John King Fisher," an unpublished article by granddaughter of Fisher.

Leakey, John (As told to Nellie Snyder Yost). *The West That Was*. Southern Methodist University Press, Dallas, 1958.

Nolen, Oran Warder. *San Antonio Express* article, reprinted in *Frontier Times* (Nov., 1949).

Roberts, Bruce. *Springs from the Parched Ground.* Hornby Press, Uvalde, Texas.

Streeter, Floyd Benjamin. *Ben Thompson: Man With a Gun.* Frederick Fell, New York, 1957.

Teel, T. T. "The Dead Desperadoes—Last of Ben Thompson and King Fisher," article in *San Antonio Express,* Mar. 13, 1884.

Walton, William M. *Life and Adventures of Ben Thompson.* Reprint ed. Frontier Press, Houston, 1954.

Wantland, Clyde. "Taking the Law to the Rio Grande," *Frontier Times* (Jan., Feb., 1936).

Books and Articles
(Secondary sources)

Adams, Paul. "The Unsolved Murder of Ben Thompson, Pistoleer Extraordinary," *The Southwestern Historical Quarterly* (July, 1945).

Cunningham, Eugene. *Triggernometry.* Press of the Pioneers, New York, 1934.

Dobie, J. Frank. *A Vaquero of the Brush Country.* Southwest Press, 1929.

———. *The Longhorns.* Bramhall House, New York, 1941.

Farrow, Marion H. *Troublesome Times in Texas.* Naylor Co., San Antonio, 1959.

Fisher, O. C. *It Occurred in Kimble.* Anson Jones Press, 1937.

Gard, Wayne. *The Chisholm Trail.* University of Oklahoma Press, Norman, 1954.

Gillette, Captain J. B. *Six Years With the Texas Rangers.* Yale University Press, New Haven, 1925.

———. "Ben Thompson and Billy Simms," *Frontier Times* (Oct., 1934).

Gregor, A. H. "Death of Ben Thompson and King Fisher," *Frontier Times* (June, 1928; Aug., 1949).

Hackett, C. W. "Recognition of the Diaz Government by the U. S.," *Southwestern Historical Quarterly* (July, 1924).

Holloway, Carroll C. *Texas Gun Lore*. Naylor Co., San Antonio, 1951.

Horn, Pat. "King Fisher," *Junior Historian*, Texas State Historical Assn. (Mar., 1952).

Hough, Emerson. *The Story of the Outlaw*. Grosset & Dunlap, New York, 1907.

Hunt, J. M., Sr. "Ben Thompson, Texas Gun Fighter," *Frontier Times* (May, 1948).

Hunter, J. Marvin. "Ben Thompson—Killer of Men," *Frontier Times* (May, 1939).

———. "Ben Thompson, Texas Gunfighter," *Frontier Times* (May, 1948).

James, Vinton Lee. *Recollections of Early Days in San Antonio and West Texas*. San Antonio, 1938.

Kilstofte, June. "Western Union," *San Antonio Express*, Sept. 30, 1951.

Lake, Stuart N. *Frontier Marshal*. Houghton, Mifflin, Boston, 1931.

Lunsford, John R. "How Ben Thompson Died With His Boots On," *Frontier Times* (Nov., 1939).

Masterson, William Barclay. *Famous Gun Fighters of the Western Frontier. Human Life*, Vol. IV (Jan., 1907).

McCoy, Joseph G. *Historical Sketches of the Cattle Trade of the West and Southwest*. Ramsey, Millett & Hudson, Kansas City, 1874.

Nordyke, Lewis. *Great Roundup*. William Morrow & Co., New York, 1955.

Pate, McNell. "Mexican Border Conflicts, 1870–80," *West Texas Historical Assn. Yearbook* (Oct., 1962).

Peyton. *City in the Sun*, San Antonio, n.d.

Ramsdell, Chas. *San Antonio*. University of Texas Press, Austin, 1959.

Sandoz, Mari. *The Cattlemen*. Hastings House, New York, 1955.

Santleben, August. *A Texas Pioneer*. Neale Publishing Co., New York, 1910.

Taylor, Paul S. "Historical Note on Dimmit County," *The Southwestern Historical Quarterly* (Oct., 1930).

Triplett, Frank. *Romance and Philosophy of Great American Crimes and Criminals*. N. D. Thompson, 1884.

Wade, Houston. *Notes and Fragments of the Mier Expedition. LaGrange Journal*, LaGrange, Tex., 1936.

Webb, Walter Prescott, ed., *A Handbook of Texas*. 2 vols. McMillan Co., 1935.

———. *The Texas Rangers*. McMillan Co., 1935.

Wilcox, Zeb S. "Address to Carrizo Springs Rotary Club of Dimmit County," *The Carrizo Springs Javelin,* Apr. 3, 1947.

Williams, Crystal S. "A History of Dimmit County," *The Carrizo Springs Javelin*, Feb. 18, 1960.

Newspapers and Magazines

Austin American, March 12, 1884, *et seq.*, covering Thompson-Fisher killing.

Austin Daily Capitol, March 12, 1884, *et seq.*, covering Thompson-Fisher killing.

Austin Daily Dispatch, March 12, 1884, *et seq.*, covering Thompson-Fisher killing.

Carrizo Springs Javelin, March 3, 10, 17, 24, and Feb. 25, 1960; April 3, 1947.

Ft. Worth Press, "Uncle Tom Sullivan," by Cal C. Huffman, Apr. 21, 1935.

Galveston News, Oct. 16, 1873; Jan. 23, 1879; Mar. 12, 13, 14, 16, 1884.

Houston Chronicle, "The House that Turned its Back on the West," an article, by Claudia Poff, Nov. 7, 1958; Dec. 21, 1924.

San Antonio Light, Mar. 26, 1950.

Uvalde Leader-News, Oct. 11, 1959.

Government Records

Collin County, Texas, court records.
General Land Office records, Austin.
Goliad County, Texas, court records.
Maverick County, Texas, court records.
Uvalde County, Texas, court records.
Webb County, Texas, court records.

Reports

36 Cong., 1 sess., *House Report 81. Troubles on the Texas Frontier.*

43 Cong., 1 sess., *House Exec. Doc. 257. Final Report of U.S. Commission to Texas, Depredations on the Frontiers of Texas*, May 26, 1874.

45 Cong., 2 sess., *House Misc. Doc. 64. Testimony Taken by Commission on Military Affairs in Relation to the Texas Border Troubles.*

45 Cong., 2 sess., *House Report 701. Report and Accompanying Documents of the Committee on Foreign Affairs on the Relations of the U.S. with Mexico.*

Texas Court of Appeals Reports, Vol. VIII, on Brazell murder case.

Texas Rangers, official reports to Adjutant General by Captains L. H. McNelly and Lee Hall (in Texas Archives, Austin), 1874–82.

U.S. Census Reports, 1850, 1860, 1870.

The Western Frontier Library

of which *King Fisher: His Life and Times* is Number 32, was started in 1953 by the University of Oklahoma Press. It is designed to introduce today's readers to the exciting events of our frontier past and to some of the memorable writings about them. The following list is complete as of the date of publication of this volume:

1. Prof. Thomas J. Dimsdale. *The Vigilantes of Montana.* With an introduction by E. DeGolyer.
2. A. S. Mercer. *The Banditti of the Plains.* With a foreword by William H. Kittrell.
3. Pat F. Garrett. *The Authentic Life of Billy, the Kid.* With an introduction by Jeff C. Dykes.
4. Yellow Bird (John Rollin Ridge). *The Life and Adventures of Joaquín Murieta.* With an introduction by Joseph Henry Jackson.
5. Lewis H. Garrard. *Wah-to-yah and the Taos Trail.* With an introduction by A. B. Guthrie, Jr.
6. Charles L. Martin. *A Sketch of Sam Bass, the Bandit.* With an introduction by Ramon F. Adams.
7. Washington Irving. *A Tour on the Prairies.* With an introduction by John Francis McDermott.
8. *X. Beidler: Vigilante.* Edited by Helen Fitzgerald Sanders in collaboration with William H. Bertsche, Jr. With a foreword by A. B. Guthrie, Jr.
9. Nelson Lee. *Three Years Among the Comanches.* With an introduction by Walter Prescott Webb.
10. *The Great Diamond Hoax and Other Stirring Incidents in the Life of Asbury Harpending.* With a foreword by Glen Dawson.
11. *Hands Up; or, Twenty Years of Detective Life in the Mountains and on the Plains:* Reminiscences by General D. J. Cook, Superintendent of the Rocky Moun-

tain Detective Association. With an introduction by Everett L. DeGolyer, Jr.

12. Will Hale. *Twenty-Four Years a Cowboy and Ranchman in Southern Texas and Old Mexico*. With an introduction by A. M. Gibson.

13. Gen. James S. Brisbin, U.S.A. *The Beef Bonanza; or, How to Get Rich on the Plains*. With a foreword by Gilbert C. Fite.

14. Isabella L. Bird. *A Lady's Life in the Rocky Mountains*. With an introduction by Daniel J. Boorstin.

15. W. T. Hamilton, *My Sixty Years on the Plains*. With an introduction by Donald J. Berthrong.

16. *The Life of John Wesley Hardin, As Written by Himself*. With an introduction by Robert G. McCubbin.

17. Elizabeth Bacon Custer. *"Boots and Saddles"; or, Life in Dakota with General Custer*. With an introduction by Jane R. Stewart.

18. John F. Finerty. *War-Path and Bivouac; or, the Conquest of the Sioux*. With an introduction by Oliver Knight.

19. Frederic Remington. *Pony Tracks*. With an introduction by J. Frank Dobie.

20. Thomas Edgar Crawford. *The West of the Texas Kid*. Edited and with an introduction by Jeff C. Dykes.

21. Frank Collinson. *Life in the Saddle*. Edited and arranged by Mary Whatley Clarke. With drawings by Harold D. Bugbee.

22. *Fifty Years on the Trail: A True Story of Western Life*. The adventures of John Young Nelson as described to Harrington O'Reilly.

23. Edward Bonney. *The Banditti of the Prairies: A Tale of the Mississippi Valley*. With an introduction by Philip D. Jordan.

24. Walter Baron von Richthofen. *Cattle-raising on the Plains of North America*. With an introduction by Edward Everett Dale.

156

The text for *King Fisher: His Life and Times* has been set on the Linotype in 10-point Times Roman, one of the most useful contemporary body types, designed by Stanley Morison of London. The paper on which this book is printed bears the University of Oklahoma Press watermark and has an effective life of at least 300 years.